MW01049531

FINDING
HAPPINESS

Sara & Mary!

God Bless!

Paul W. Sweets

11-10-15

FINDING HAPPINESS

BUILDING STABLE RELATIONSHIPS IN TURBULENT TIMES

Paul W. Swets

CROSSLINK
PUBLISHING

Finding Happiness: Building Stable Relationships In Turbulent Times

CrossLink Publishing
www.crosslinkpublishing.com

Copyright, © 2015 Paul W. Swets

All rights reserved. No part of this book may be reproduced in any form, except for brief quotations in reviews, without the written permission of the author.

Printed in the United States of America. All rights reserved under International Copyright Law.

ISBN 978-1-63357-036-8

Library of Congress Control Number: 2015942987

Other books by Paul W. Swets:

The Art of Talking So That People Will Listen, Simon & Schuster, 1992

The Art of Talking With Your Teenager, Adams Media, 1995, CreateSpace, 2015.

Dreaming BIG, coauthored with Bobb Biehl, Authentic Press, 2007

READER REVIEWS

"Who wouldn't like to be happy and the best person you could possibly be? Every one of us has this deep-seated desire for happiness and fulfillment. *Finding Happiness* is fantastic! It should be another winner. Paul has a unique insight of how we can experience joy and purpose. And like a good head coach, he gives us the tools to accomplish this. Read *Finding Happiness*. It's transformational!" **C. Kemmons Wilson, Jr., Founding Family of Holiday Inns**

"A refreshing read. *Finding Happiness* is so well written—clear, articulate, engaging. It is packed full of wisdom about how to live this life well. It is a right-on gift of a book." **Mark Hiskes, Teacher**

"A brilliantly sequenced menu of solutions for every person's core need to be happy now and joyous forever! Paul clearly identifies the inherent resources every person already has to love, to submit to God, and to celebrate life as it is meant to be! Destined to be a classic—thanks, Paul." **Kyle Rote, Jr., National Soccer Hall of Fame**

"*Finding Happiness* is filled with wisdom, wit, and great take-away ideas to strengthen each of our relationships. Both my wife and I kept saying, 'This is a great book!'" **Jim Carlson, author of *Choosing to be Fully Alive***

"I think this book is exceptional! *Finding Happiness* has a lot to offer everyone in terms of acquiring the skills for successful communication and conflict resolution. These skills are so necessary to be effective in life. People of all ages will benefit from them." **Harrison C. Visscher, MD**

"*Finding Happiness* offers a powerfully written set of tools that sparks action. It encourages, challenges, and ultimately inspires us to make the necessary changes in our lives to allow true happiness to endure. Paul Swets teaches us that life is worth celebrating! So why not start today by connecting, relating, mentoring, and choosing to persevere with hope. I know *Finding Happiness* will impact the lives of many!" **Jenna Grasmeyer, 2014 NCAA Division III Volleyball Championship's Most Outstanding Player**

"*Finding Happiness* offers helpful insight for living a happy life. With a clear intelligence and gentle tone, Paul Swets mentors us about how to connect with those around us, how to develop a life of depth and purpose, and how to live today without fear of tomorrow. His skill and compassion shine through every page of this profound little book." **Alex Mouw, Lilly Graduate Fellow**

"As an artist I spend a lot of alone time, stuck in my head. When I venture out from my studio I crave conversation and interaction that matters. As Paul Swets thoroughly lays out in *Finding Happiness,* it really comes down to relationships that matter. If you're willing to truly engage with this book, I think you'll find reason to venture out from whatever your personal 'studio' may be because a fuller life is waiting for you." **Joel Schoon-Tanis, Artist**

"*Finding Happiness* is a gold mine of coaching strategies for enjoying an abundant life. As a recent college graduate, I find the principles spot on and immediately accessible by my generation. This book fills the gap in our culture by showing the way to enduring happiness." **Sa'eed Hussaini, Research Intern at the Center for Strategic and International Studies**

"I believe *Finding Happiness* will be a practical resource for family and marriage counselors, and for people who want to improve their interpersonal relationships. This is a self-help book that is easy to read, practical in its application, sound in its principles, and appropriate for all ages." **Harold Gazan, MSW, former consultant to Child Welfare and Juvenile Justice Agencies**

"*Finding Happiness* brings together not only the necessary practices to initiate and develop lasting friendship, but a reason to even develop these friendships in the first place. The effort laid out here for friendship and happiness is beautiful." **Jeff Miller, Engineer**

"Motivating! I like this fresh approach for opening ways to get through to people and create a happy experience." **Courtney Dykema, College Graduate**

"Drawing upon his doctoral research in interpersonal communication in his newest book, Dr. Paul Swets helps you maximize your communication skills and build satisfying relationships." **Bobb Biehl, Executive Mentor**

DEDICATION

To Janiece, my wife and best friend, and mother of
our two children, Judson and Jessica,
and one who daily multiplies my happiness.

CONTENTS

YOU CAN EXPERIENCE LASTING HAPPINESS!

Preface

Who doesn't want to be happy? The US Declaration of Independence calls "the pursuit of happiness" an inalienable right. *Time* magazine describes the desire for happiness as *built in*.[1]

If we are "wired" for it, why haven't we made more progress toward a satisfaction that lasts?

Most of us want to laugh more often, to have friends who care about us, to live purpose-filled lives, to have a calm center even when others are panicky. Yet even minor irritations can easily derail happiness. Why is that?

You have reasons for unhappiness. So do I. We can't escape bad times. Betrayed trust, major disappointments, missed opportunities, personal suffering—these rough seasons are part of life. They make happiness elusive for many. We know money can't buy lasting happiness.[2] Celebrity news often shows that popularity doesn't bring happiness. Landing a job or earning a college degree may bring only short-lived satisfaction.

Social psychologist David Myers, author of *The Pursuit of Happiness,* summarizes our unsuccessful efforts:

We excel at making a living but fail at making a life.
We celebrate our prosperity but yearn for purpose.
We cherish our freedoms but long for connection.
In an age of plenty, we feel spiritually hungry.[3]

What value is it if you are popular but have no one to call a true friend? What does it matter if you are prosperous but feel an emptiness in your soul? The fact is we want happiness, but we don't know how to find it.

Is help available? Can people truly expect to find deep contentment and delight? If so, how?

Happiness results from building stable relationships.

My research shows that while we were made to relate to others, we find it terribly difficult. Relationships are a fundamental human problem. Although it might be easier to function alone (we don't have to explain, convince, argue, or consider someone else's feelings), study in psychology and American culture overwhelmingly supports the notion that we are *social* beings. We need to find ways to get through to people if we want to be happy. And that's where we'll begin.

Robert Holden, author of *Happiness Now*, reported in a BBC documentary that "the proportion of people saying they are 'very happy' has fallen from 52 percent in 1957 to just 36 percent" in 2006.[4] Why?

Many researchers have offered helpful explanations and suggestions for attaining happiness.[5] We will gladly draw upon their wisdom. But in this little book, we focus on tools you can use to relate better with friends and family by fine-tuning your communication skills. We'll move from communicating better with each other to communicating better with God, which will invigorate our souls. The result? Real, lasting, irresistible happiness!

Finding Happiness provides four tools for building strong relationships: Friendship, Connection, Purpose, and Hope. What you build with these can help you withstand the stormy times in life and change the way you approach everyday living.

Friendship tools (Chapters 1–3) help you build bridges of relationship. You'll discover how to attract people to you via smart listening and talking. As your relationship coach, I'll help you practice these skills so you can establish satisfying friendships. Good friends enable you to create, share, and thus multiply happiness.

Connection tools (Chapters 4–6) help you become more deeply connected with caring people. Professor Ed Diener, aka "the happiness doctor," studied some of the happiest people in various parts of the world and found that "all of them had close, supportive family and friends."[6] Isn't it true that when you fail to communicate skillfully, you feel disconnected and alone? What would it mean to you if you could reduce emotional distance with friends and family by resolving disagreements, sustaining worthwhile friendships, and creating deeper understanding? Although you can't control how others relate to you, you can ensure that you communicate in a way that makes others want to be with you. Understanding among friends helps you feel more connected, more resilient, more sturdy. Being well connected helps you gain a positive perspective (and get happy!).

Purpose tools (Chapters 7–8) help you enjoy a meaningful life in two ways: by *giving back to others*—passing on your knowledge to someone who can learn from your experience, and by *moving forward*—crafting your own mission statement in one sentence. These tools energize you for life and help you flourish.

Hope tools (chapters 9–10) help you renew your mind through a transforming relationship with God. Your mind can be worn down by anxiety about what *might* happen, frustration about goals not met, and weariness from the constant demands of life. Renewing your mind reverses that trend by transforming you on the inside. It prepares your mind for hope that endures, so that even in a chaotic world, you experience a harmony of understanding, closeness, giving-back-gratitude, and optimism. That's called finding happiness!

To summarize: through this book, I will show that happiness will be found when you

- communicate skillfully
- relate in depth with people
- make a difference in peoples' lives as well as your own.
- live life filled with enduring hope in God, the stable center in our often chaotic relationships

Friend, if you have tried to achieve happiness by unsuccessful means, you may feel trapped by past mistakes. Yet I believe no effort and no mistake—or even matters beyond your choice such as background or upbringing—is unusable in the realignment of your life. Your challenge and mine is to manage well what we can choose. I'll show you how.

Will you join me? Then let's get started. Happiness awaits!

PART ONE:
BUILDING FRIENDSHIPS

Wishing to be friends is quick work, but friendship is a slow ripening fruit.

—Aristotle

Aristotle confirms our experience—friendship takes time. But it yields the exceptional taste of a slowly ripened fruit.

Part One of *Finding Happiness* guides you through the ripening process of becoming a good friend—someone other people want to know. You build friendships by knowing how to use these communication tools:

- how to attract people
- how to listen
- how to talk so people will listen to you

My job is to serve as your personal mentor; to come alongside and show you how these communication tools help you find happiness. You and your new friends will be glad you made the effort!

ATTRACT PEOPLE TO YOU

Chapter 1

*A true friend is someone who thinks that you are
a good egg even though he knows that you are
slightly cracked.*

—Bernard Meltzer

H ave you ever wondered why people consistently are drawn to a colleague or acquaintance even when that "center of attention" is not all that good-looking or well-dressed or highly educated? What's going on? What's the appeal?

Communication skills that attract! When the "center of attention" speaks, she smiles at you and confidently looks you in the eye. She asks questions that show she really wants to know what you think. She attracts people because she builds bridges for relationship.

With a strong relational bridge, you can share your thoughts and feelings in a way that attracts others to you. Relational attraction does not depend primarily on popularity with the "in" crowd. You don't need to be perfect. In fact, sooner or later people will realize you're "slightly cracked"—most of us are!

Just as you are, cracks and all, you can draw people to you if you work on a few people skills. Attraction involves how effective you are as a communicator. The way you get through to people is the bridge by which they get through to you.

This chapter focuses on general communication principles and offers tools to connect with those you want to know better. The exciting fact is that even if you are slightly cracked, there are at least four ways you can draw people to you. Take a look.

Tool 1: Ask Good Questions

Perhaps you have had to endure monotonous conversations where others talk only about themselves. You can help make the time enjoyable by asking good questions. Here's why they work. Good questions:

- Enable you and the other person to talk about mutually satisfying topics.
- Convey respect for your companions' ideas.

Warning: not all questions are *good* questions. Bad questions, asked only for the purpose of giving your own opinions or drawing attention to yourself (e.g., "What did you think of my performance?"), shut the door to better understanding. The listener feels used, not affirmed. Constant questioning also can make your friends uneasy. They wonder, *Why the inquisition?* Good questions keep your companion in mind. They don't intimidate. They don't make the person feel awkward or invaded. They don't stop the flow of communication—they start it!

Before we develop the skill of asking good questions, let's look at a few bad ones to avoid.

- Are you out of your mind? (Judgmental)
- What do you think should be done about the immigration crisis? (Complicated)
- What did you say? (Implies you're not listening)
- Why is there so much racial intolerance in our town? (Troubling topic)

Have you asked questions that clearly made your companion uncomfortable or defensive? Has anyone ever shut down a conversation with you out of boredom? Even if you recognize in yourself a habit of asking the wrong kind of questions, the kind that repel people, you can learn to ask good ones and draw people in. You can make effective adjustments in your conversational style by using the following techniques.

Reduce Implied Threat

Emotions may be involved in your conversation. Even a simple question may suggest a subtle threat. Your friend wonders, *Will you use the information you are asking for against me? Why do you need that information? Are you going to judge me by how I answer this question?* Reduce threat by making your purpose clear. For example, you can say:

- Just for my information…
- I'm trying to decide what car to buy and I'd like your opinion.
- I'm interested in your thoughts on a decision I'm trying to make.

- Honey, our checkbook balance is very low. What can we do to cut our costs?

Stating your purpose clarifies your intentions and breaks down defenses.

Ask Simple Questions First

With a new person, begin with nonthreatening questions that call for a yes or no answer. "Do you like this weather?" Then you can move to open-ended questions that draw out the other person's thoughts. "What do you like about your new job?"

Listen Prudently

Listen to other people's tone of voice and even how fast they answer. Consider not only the meaning of their words, but what the words imply. This extra information helps you know how best to respond. For example, reticence to discuss a topic might suggest there is something more to the topic that your friend wants to share but he is not sure how you'll handle it. You might say, "I notice you are hesitant to talk about this. Would you rather talk about something else?" or "Am I missing something?" or "Does this bring up some thoughts you would like to share?"

Beware of Troublesome Topics

Sometimes we get carried away talking about our favorite issues. But what interests us sometimes generates more emotional distance than understanding. To attract friends, avoid questions that put the respondent on the spot or incite a heated reply such as "You're judging me!" "I'm not stupid!" "It sounds like I'm on trial for something!" To repair the conversation bridge, you can say, "I'm sorry that what I said troubles you. I didn't mean to imply any judgment."

When you ask good questions

- you earn the right to be heard by taking the time to listen.
- you meet other people's needs for attention and give them a chance to tell their stories.
- you may learn something new!
- you establish rapport and strengthen friendship—which increases happiness.

People are normally honored when you care enough to ask about their thoughts or achievements. You attract them to you.

Tool 2: Learn How to Start Conversations

We've all been there: someone next to us seems friendly, intelligent, lively, and we'd like to start a chat...but we're not sure where to begin. We don't want to be overpowering or overly meek, but what do we do?

It can be difficult to begin a satisfying conversation. But almost without exception, people like to talk if they feel the listener really wants to hear. Unfortunately, some people are so starved for attention that if you give them an opening, they'll gladly take more time than you have to give. You may have to halt the nonstop talker by inserting your thoughts at an opportune moment or asking a question of another person in your group, redirecting attention and giving another a chance to talk. Still, the possible benefits of being a conversation starter are worth the risk.

If you carry a bevy of conversation starters in your mind, you'll wield a major tool in attracting others to you. Here are a few worth committing to memory. In appropriate settings, they are likely to jump-start meaningful discussion.

- What first attracted you to your line of work?
- If you could do any kind of work, what would it be?
- What do you like or dislike about your job?
- What would you like to do or achieve next year?
- If you won the lottery, what would you do with all the money?
- If you could be any person at any time in history, who would that be?
- What issues concern you?
- Whom do you most admire? Why?
- What sports or hobbies do you enjoy?
- Tell me about your children.

Add to this list questions related to your own special interests or line of work. Answers will lead to follow-up questions. Remember, the aim is not to contradict or disagree with the answers you get, but to appreciate your companion's viewpoint. Ask questions without a judgmental attitude. Focus on making conversation interesting, mutual, and fun. People are attracted to those conversations.

Tool 3: Avoid Conversation Stoppers

Think for a moment about various people in your experience who make conversation difficult. What do they do or say that causes the problem? Is it incessant talking, complaining, a whiney tone of voice? Is it their mannerisms or attitudes? Are they withdrawn or shy?

Avoid responses that turn off the flow of conversation. Here are some examples:

- Don't think that way!
- I know exactly how you feel!
- That's a stupid idea!
- Are you out of your mind?
- That's not the way it's done!
- Are you deaf?
- You're wrong!

To detect ways you might stop conversations, check yourself on each of the following and take special notice where you need to improve. Or better yet, ask someone you trust to honestly evaluate you. For any question your friend answers with a yes, ask for an example from your life. Look at this as an opportunity for personal growth.

_____ Is my voice too loud?
_____ Do I have a habit of complaining?
_____ Do I tend to be critical of people?
_____ Is the tone of my voice annoying?
_____ Do I sound as if I don't care?
_____ Do I give the other person equal talk time?
_____ Do I focus attention on myself?
_____ Do I sound condescending or argumentative?
_____ Do I mumble when I talk?
_____ Do I boss people around?
_____ Do I talk too much about my work?

_____ Do I drone on and on?

_____ Do I sound "holier than thou"?

_____ Do I cut off other people when they're trying to talk?

If the answer to any of these questions is yes, be encouraged! Your awareness of a problem is the first step in fixing it. My problem was retelling the same stories or jokes over and over. Then it dawned on me what I was doing. My wife confirmed it. I decided to change by turning my attention on my friends and asking a memorized conversation starter.

When you make necessary changes in your conversation patterns, you reduce serious blunders that drive people apart. I appreciate the help my wife gives in this regard when she helps direct the conversation to a more positive outcome. For example, she might ask, "How could you have said that better?" Write that question down! Ask yourself that question the split second before you let loose with an angry outburst. It will help you say what you want to say, but without hurting anyone. Avoiding conversation stoppers enables you to make adjustments that will attract people to you.

Tool 4: Think Twice

Perhaps a parent or teacher cautioned you to *think* before speaking. They were half right. I would add that you need to think twice: first about *what* you want to say, and second about *how* to say it so that your thought gets through but doesn't blow your friends away. Sounds hard, but don't sell your brain short. It works faster than the speed of sound. In a split second, you can change your word selection and tone of voice to be more appealing.

Ask yourself *what* will interest the other person. Sports? Issues of the day? Practice looking at an idea or problem from your companion's point of view. Mentally play out an idea to see its short- and long-range consequences. Treat ideas as potential friends. Don't be afraid to explore new topics that are of interest to your respondent, such as who will win in the Final Four in basketball or what contestant will win in the TV program *America's Got Talent*.

Then consider *how* you will convey your message. For example, suppose your impulse in discussing some topic is to blurt out, "That will never work!" but in that second before you talk, you ask yourself, *How could I say that better?* Immediately you change your outburst to a question: "How do you see that working?" The first message may be a conversation stopper; the second is definitely a conversation starter.

As you think twice about how to attract people to you, consider:

1. What do my tone of voice and facial expression convey? Do I sound or look angry or cheerful? Does my face convey acceptance, anxiety, or disapproval?
2. Will what I say and how I'm about to say it repel or attract?

Asking yourself these questions can help you make winsome modifications that attract people to you. If your relational bridge is strong and if you and your friends like to have friendly debates, share your deeper thoughts and feelings, even when they differ from prevailing opinion. Develop an attractive balance between being overly assertive and maintaining openness by following up your statement with a question: "Is that right?" "What do you think?" Memorize small chunks of information on topics you find interesting. You can become a brilliant conversationalist when you glean even one topic from the newspaper or Internet on a regular basis and then assert your opinions when appropriate.

For example, you're at a restaurant with a few friends. The conversation turns to sports and you say, "I'm concerned about all the head concussions in football. I'm not sure the fun of the sport is worth the danger. What do you all think?" Or you say, "When I listen to news reports about a deadly virus, I wonder what would motivate so many people to go to an infected area and offer their help. I don't know if I could do that. Could you?"

These tools are necessary to build a strong relational bridge:

- Ask good questions
- Learn how to start conversations
- Avoid conversation stoppers
- Think twice.

Whether you talk about basketball or jogging, music or current events, your favorite movie or the economy, your thoughts and feelings will be of interest because they represent you. You reveal that you care about other people's ideas. You add value to someone's life by asking for and appreciating his or her opinion. You attract others to you. You begin to experience more happiness.

LISTEN SO PEOPLE TALK

Chapter 2

*Listening is a magnetic and strange thing, a
creative force. The friends who listen to us are the
ones we move toward.*

—Karl Menninger

M arcus came to see me for counsel, but was not able to talk about what was troubling him. He seemed as though he didn't want to be there. He wore a grim expression and appeared restless. Yet I knew he had something to say. So I persisted, using six listening actions that eventually motivated him to tell me what was worrying him.

You too can encourage your friends to level with you when you listen skillfully. Consider the benefits of having people who talk to you because you listen well:

- Loneliness reverses—you and your companion feel more connected.
- Belonging is confirmed—you feel part of your social group.
- Understanding increases—you feel enriched.
- Companionship surges—you feel you are with a friend.

I find myself moving toward those who really listen to me. Likewise, I want to be the kind of person who draws people I care about to me. Why? In addition to the benefits I've just listed, building friendships through listening enables me to break free from mind-numbing self-preoccupation. Caring about others makes me more compelling to others and a better communicator. It increases my happiness.

Are you a good listener? Here's a simple test:

- Do people talk with you easily?
- Do they seem eager to tell you what's on their minds?
- Do they trust you enough to talk about topics that might not be considered "safe"?
- Do they appear to enjoy being with you?

If you answered yes to any of these questions, you're on the right track. If you answered any of these with a no, this chapter will expose you to some listening practices you will want to learn because they are like magnets that draw people to you.

1. Listen to Yourself

You may think this an odd recommendation, but do you adequately listen to yourself? Do you know what you really think? Do you pay attention to your own big dreams or ambitions? If you don't, you aren't giving yourself the benefit of knowing what you think. This in turn makes you more hesitant about engaging in a conversation and listening well to another.

I can hear you say to yourself, "Good idea! I'd love to reflect on my dreams and hopes for the future, but I never seem to find the time. *How* can I listen to myself?" Here are a few suggestions I've found helpful:

- Schedule time to reflect about what you think and feel on two or three current issues: *Where do I want my relationship with George to go? What will I say to my boss who is asking me to cheat? What do my children need from me right now?*
- Ask yourself questions to draw out your thoughts: *What do I want to accomplish in my work? Am I pursuing my life purpose? How do I want to respond to Fred's suggestion?*
- Journal your thoughts, even if it's just a sentence or two, to gain clarity.

Listening carefully to yourself enables you to hear what others hear. You can identify what you need to change. For example, would parents change their tone if they really listened to themselves talking to their children? Would there be less harsh language?

As you understand how you come across to others, you might identify tendencies you want to change. When you are aware of a deficiency, you can take steps to correct it. Corrective action will help you to replace negative habits that push people away with positive behaviors that draw others closer. For example, when you listen to yourself, you may be surprised to hear an unpleasant tone in your voice. If you then consciously try to modulate your voice, you can make it sound more accepting, more pleasing, more easy on the ear.

Listen to yourself in order to better listen to others.

2. Overcome Barriers to Listening

If you've discovered you're not a good listener, you can *change*. You can choose to listen fully! As I will explain more in chapter nine, you actually have the capability of choice. You can *choose* to overcome poor listening habits and eliminate some listening distractions. Let's focus on three barriers to friendship-building that need to be overcome.[1]

Stress

You probably know the damaging effects stress has on the body. Heart attacks, strokes, accidents, plus numerous other ailments have all been attributed, at least in part, to stress. But did you know that relationships also are affected? A stressed-out person doesn't focus well or give full attention to another person. Friends know when your mind is somewhere else. They can see it in shifty eyes, a bored look, restlessness. Avoid stress by getting adequate rest, minimizing distractions, setting a time later to focus on your "to-do list," and reminding yourself to be calm. Then you'll be freer to listen.

The "Me" Syndrome

American youth used to be known as the "Me Generation." Now *Time* magazine designates millennials as the "Me, Me, Me Generation."[2] Humans show a fundamental tendency toward self-centeredness. That's evident when people listen only to what will benefit them and tune out the rest. I do this sometimes, letting the "Me Syndrome" block the goal of communication—full understanding.

Are you too self-absorbed? To find out, answer these questions:

- In most conversations, what percentage of time do you talk about your own concerns and what percentage of time do you listen? Is there a balance?
- Do you commonly ask questions to draw out the thoughts of the other person?

Sometimes our egos are like boomerangs: initially we may appear to show interest in other people, only to curve the conversation back to ourselves, revealing that we're truly interested only in ourselves. When your purpose in relationships is limited to what you can get out of them, you tend not to show genuine care about the thoughts or feelings of others. Relationships dissipate, friends feel used. When you ask questions about your friend's engagement, promotion, or new job—and then sincerely listen—they know you're interested in them.

Brain Speed

While an average speech rate is about 200 words per minute, most of us can think about 800 words per minute.[3] So what do our brains do with all that extra time? Wander! "To do" lists! Think about a personal problem! It makes effective listening impossible. If friends notice you're easily distracted, they will feel you don't think they are important enough to hold your attention. They'll stop talking. Use your extra brain speed to benefit the relationship by:

- Listening for implications beyond the words. When your friend says, "I had a miserable day today," you can follow up by saying "Tell me what happened."
- Choosing a thoughtful, wise, or kind response to what's being said.

Choosing to focus attention on the other person helps you tear down barriers that block conversation.

3. Listen Dynamically

Dynamic listening is taking part in a conversation so that the other person knows you care about what he is saying. You concentrate on what is being said, ask questions, and sometimes repeat in your own words what a person has said to make sure you understand.

Your friends know you are listening dynamically when you give simple responses that show you are fully engaged in the conversation:

- So, what you're saying is…
- I never thought of that before.
- Tell me what you are thinking.
- Tell me how you feel about this.
- Let's discuss it.
- What else are you thinking?
- I like the way you think.
- Should we brainstorm some ideas to fix that problem?

Responses like these help you to better understand what your friends are saying. As you master this skill, you increase mutual understanding. People enjoy talking to you.

4. Listen for Concepts and Motives

Often we half-listen to small talk. But sometimes small talk encases strong ideas and significant feelings. A husband watching football half-listened to what he thought was small talk and really fumbled the ball (pun intended). His wife said, "You know, I think I might be getting sick." He replied, "Sounds good."

Small talk has its place in social conversation; it breaks the ice and lets people exchange bits of information. But we don't listen to a TV commercial with the same intensity as we do when someone special says, "I love you." Awareness of the following types of communication helps determine when to listen harder for ideas and feelings.

Banalities

These are phrases without much meaning: "It's all good." "Awesome." "All's well that ends well." "How is it going?" As agents of minimum politeness, they can still facilitate conversation and lead to better conversation. When you ask, "How are you?" and your friend replies, "I've had a hard week!" you can show genuine interest by putting your active listening skills to work. To encourage further conversation, you might ask, "Hard week? How so?"

Evidences

These generally refer to something that is verifiable. "The temperature will reach 90 degrees today." "Many people have not saved enough money for retirement." Sharing of facts might lead to the next level of discussing one's thoughts about the topic. "Do you think Social Security will be viable when you retire?"

Opinions

These represent our interpretation of facts or events: "I think the weather patterns have been weird the past few years." "Teachers should be paid more because the good ones influence the whole trajectory of a student's life." "Jessica has the heart and skill to motivate special education kids to do things they never thought possible." These statements invite agreement or disagreement—which can deepen a conversation and thus, a relationship.

Feelings

When intense feelings are expressed, we have a choice how we will respond. For example, someone might assert with a tone of outrage, "I feel women are still being discriminated against!" As a listener, you may not be sure how to handle conversation full of emotion. Not wanting to hurt a person's feelings, you might pull back to a safer, more superficial level.

But here's the problem: when we refuse to listen and respond to ideas and feelings, our companions may do the same. Conversations then degenerate into superficial mumbling.

You need to be mentally strong enough to listen to emotional outbursts or raw opinions without immediately trying to fix or change anything. Here are some listening principles that help when emotions are high.

- Refuse to evaluate, judge, or condemn ("You're prejudiced!" "You don't make sense.")
- When you feel judged, tell your friend, "Hey, let's agree not to judge each other. I'm just offering an opinion. Let's discuss the pros and cons. Okay?"
- Aim to understand, not control. Respond with "Why?" instead of "No one in their right mind thinks that way."
- Accept the expression of deep feeling as possibly valid, but maybe not the whole truth. "I understand you're upset right now. Let's talk more about this later."

- Tell your friend if you need a break from a difficult emotional conversation. Then set a mutually acceptable time to continue if you both think it would be worthwhile.

Feelings change, sometimes in a moment. What she says in a fit of anger may be completely contrary to her real values. Be secure enough to withstand an emotional onslaught and enable the other person to see the bigger picture by asking, "Is that what you really believe?" or "Have you always felt this way?" It takes courage and patience, but it's a sign of real friendship when you help the other put into words what he's feeling.

> Jennifer: Men are mere animals!
> Brad: Have you always felt this way?
> Jennifer: Didn't you see what he did?
> Brad: Yes. There's absolutely no excuse for his behavior! But Jenny, does that mean all men are like that?
> Jennifer: No, I guess not. You're not.

Listen for ideas and feelings. Your companions will talk freely when they know you care about what's important to them. A relationship is sparked—as is happiness!

5. Listen for Sound and Meaning

Pay attention to the sound of one's voice. Listening with the *ear* is an amazing physiological process by which the ears receive auditory impressions and transmit them to the brain. Studies show that your outer ear, sculptured like a sound trumpet, catches sound waves and guides them into the auditory canal. At the end of the canal, the waves vibrate the eardrum, sending vibrations across the three bones of the middle ear and moving the innermost bone in and out. Then a fluid translates sound waves into nerve impulses and stimulates nerves to send messages to the hearing center of the brain. Auditory scientists have discovered recently that ability to discern pitch hinges on extraordinary gradations in cells within the inner ear.[4] Remarkable!

Listening for meaning refers to an even more complex psychological process that involves interpreting and understanding the significance of the sensory experience. In *The Art of Talking So That People Will* Listen, I write, "A baby's cry, the roar of the ocean, powerful symphonic music, an inspiring speech—these and other sounds produce within us feelings, thoughts, and actions that can immeasurably enrich our lives."[5]

When we listen for meaning, we respond to the sounds we hear according to what we value. For example, if we value the sound of music, listening to a concert can be exciting, even moving. In fact, such listening reflects the meaning of the word—to *list* means, among other things, to lean forward. When we lean toward the person we're listening to, we show we are emotionally, mentally, and even physically inclined to get the full meaning of what he is saying. Friends can see in our posture we are listening with our hearts. They are encouraged. The conversation grows. Friendship deepens.

To increase our ability to listen with the heart, we need to cultivate two interpersonal qualities—empathy and acceptance. *Empathy* is putting ourselves in the other person's place and asking, *How would I feel in that situation?* It's trying to understand the other as fully as possible. When trying to show empathy, you might say, "I'm ready to listen. I really want to understand what you're saying."

Acceptance is conveying to others that they are valuable just as they are. They don't need to prove their value to us or meet a certain set of standards. You may ask: What if the other person says or does something I don't like? Ask yourself: Do I dislike the *person* or the *action*? There is a great difference between thinking that a *person* is a failure and that his *actions* have resulted in failure. Focus your attitudes on acceptance of the person in spite of behavior that is unacceptable.

- We just went through that red light! I know that's not the way you normally drive. What are you thinking about?
- I don't like it when you criticize me in front of my friends. How can we show instead how much we support each other?

When you listen with your heart, the other person will more likely talk because she doesn't feel condemned or judged. Listen with your heart if you want others to talk.

6. Know When Not to Speak

As a counselor, I had to learn that keeping my mouth shut was sometimes the best response. If a client is grieving, for example, few words are truly helpful. If a client is testing me to see if I really want to hear what he has to say, my staying silent and calmly looking at him with acceptance tells him I'm ready and waiting for him to talk. I have learned to "read" the other person's facial expressions (tense or relaxed face) and body language (arms folded or leaning toward me) to discern if a person really wants to talk. If I'm not sure, I've found it best to wait quietly or ask an open-ended question like, "What are you thinking or feeling right now?"

I'm amazed at the healing effect of someone giving full attention in supportive silence. Perhaps you, too, have experienced the conversational gift when a loved one exercised the discipline of silently hearing you out instead of contradicting or trying to fix what you think. I know I've judiciously listened to someone when she says, "Thanks for listening! I know now what I need to do." What did I do? What insights did I offer that brought a sense of calmness and direction? Very little. I simply listened in attentive silence. You can, too.

The most common and serious error a person makes is trying to solve the problem for a friend. Ask yourself if you tend to be too ready to give advice, instruction, logic, or "answers" in hopes of relieving a friend's confusion or emotional struggle. Ask a close friend, "Do I tend to talk too much or at the wrong time? Please be candid with me. I really want to know."

Rather than responding with "answers," maybe the other person is most helped when you know how he feels. Maybe he needs you to just listen. Healing happens best when you help your friends discover their own answers by asking relevant questions or just letting them think out loud.

Let me give you a real-life example. In the course of several years, the Bayly family lost three of their children. In *The Last Thing We Talk About*, Joe Bayly shared his feelings about two friends who tried to help when one of his children died.

> *I was sitting, torn by grief. Someone came and talked to me of God's dealings, of why it happened, of hope beyond the grave. He talked constantly. He said things I knew were true.*
> *I was unmoved, except to wish he'd go away. He finally did.*
> *Another came and sat beside me. He didn't talk. He didn't ask me leading questions. He just sat beside me for an hour and more, listened when I said something, answered briefly, prayed simply, left. I was moved. I was comforted. I hated to see him go."*[6]

Your supportive silence can make a difference to people in crisis. You will need to be mentally disciplined; you don't need to answer every question.

Developing your skills in listening can change your life and that of your friends. Nothing matches the deep satisfaction in your companions when you use the tool of listening well. You grow relationships; you find happiness.

TALK SO PEOPLE LISTEN

Chapter 3

Shut up and talk!

—Yogi Berra

ave you witnessed or participated in conversations where people are talking at each other, but no communication is really happening? Perhaps no one is saying anything worth listening to. Former New York Yankees baseball player Yogi Berra, known for saying whatever was on his mind, was fed up with chatter on his team when he blurted out his famous one-liner: "Shut up and talk!"[1]

Although talking comes naturally, getting people to listen requires talking so that they *want* to listen to you. To be successful, we need to make slight adjustments in choosing the right thoughts, the right tone, the right time, and the right words.

Some time ago, David Leestma, my astronaut cousin flying on the *Challenger*, answered a question about navigation. He explained that only slight adjustments were needed to keep the space shuttle on track. But if those adjustments were ignored, the shuttle would wander millions of miles from its destination. The same is true in relationships. Small course corrections in what you say enable you to talk so people listen.

Talking successfully is not rocket science. But it is a matter of knowing what interests your friends and making a few skillful adjustments to keep you and them on the same page. You might be thinking, *Do I really have to think about talking? I've been talking since birth! By now I should be an expert!* Well, sure. Experience and intuition help, but for some below-the-surface reason, we've got a fundamental problem in connecting with others: everyone talks about himself or herself; no one listens. It's a conversation problem that needs a course correction.

In this chapter, we outline communication principles that control what we say and how we listen. Ask yourself to what degree your conversation is directed by these seven qualities. Identify areas you may need to work on that will increase your happiness.

Self-Awareness

In chapter two, I wrote that listening to yourself helps you listen better to others. Similarly, self-awareness helps you adjust the way you talk so others find it interesting to listen to you.

How well do you really know yourself? As a graduate student at the University of Michigan, I remember peers asking the question, *"Who am I?"* It's not as senseless as it might appear. Parents, relatives, and friends may all try to squeeze us into their mold. Sometimes we make ourselves unhappy by trying to please someone else. Who we really are and what we are ideally suited for in life becomes blurred.

To check your self-awareness, rate how often the following statements are true for you. Better yet, consider asking a trusted friend to rate you on these things. Choose the word that best represents the frequency of each item in your experience (Seldom, Sometimes, Often, or Usually). It will help you find out where you may need to improve.

Seldom / Sometimes / Often / Usually

- I'm aware of the emotions I feel.
- I'm aware of my voice tone and gestures.
- People appear to feel comfortable listening to me.
- My word choice attracts rather than repels others.
- I notice the impact of my thoughts and feelings.

If you answered Seldom or Sometimes to any or all of these statements, you can choose to focus your attention more in these areas in order to improve self-awareness. By paying attention to *how* you talk, you cultivate an ongoing consciousness about yourself that helps you know what you need to work on to relate effectively with others. Remember that you can change if you want to. You can become a person others like to be around. You can become more skillful at sharing your viewpoint *and* being open to the insights of others.

Janiece, my wife, finds it helps to remind herself of who she is becoming through self-affirmations that identify her goal and the hoped-for result:

> *I am becoming the person I want to be. I'm choosing values and beliefs that define my thinking and how I relate to others. People feel comfortable listening to me because they can see in my facial expression that I sincerely care about them.*

Self-awareness is essential to getting people to listen.

Understanding

In *The Art of Talking So That People Will Listen,* I tell one of my favorite stories about a professor who wanted his students to understand the damaging effects of drinking alcohol. To dramatize the effect, he placed a worm in a glass of water and another in a glass of gin. He showed the class how the glass of water had no detrimental effect on the worm, but that the worm in the glass of gin promptly died and all but dissolved. With a confident look on his face, he asked, "Now, what does that prove to you?" From the back of the room, a student retorted, "If you drink alcohol, you won't have worms!"[2]

Sometimes people intentionally misinterpret what we say. Other times people sincerely have difficulty knowing the meaning we intend. Exasperated by a friend's misinterpretation, one person quipped, "I know you believe you understand what you think I said, but I am not sure you realize that what you heard is not what I meant!"

When you sense that the person you are talking with has misinterpreted your message, ask clarifying questions like, "How do you respond to that idea?" or "Do you know what I mean?" Then wait for the answer. By asking clarifying questions like these, you are able to correct misinterpretations and avoid wrong assumptions.

Misunderstanding is difficult to prevent when we don't know why it occurs. To better identify causes of misunderstanding, communication expert Albert Mehrabian studied what impacts a message. Before we look at his results, what do you estimate is the relative impact of your *words, tone,* and *posture* in getting your message across? Write in your guesses below so that the total is 100 percent.

Words affect_____ % of my communication.

Tone affects_____ % of my communication.

Facial expression affects_____% of my communication.

Here are the results from the study: Words (verbal) 7 percent; Tone (vocal) 38 percent; Facial expression (visual) 55 percent.[3] Surprised? Me too! How do your own estimates compare with the professor's?

What are the implications of Mehrabian's figures for how you talk? Is it possible that your words say one thing, but your tone of voice or posture says something different? What area might you need to improve to increase understanding?

I know we need to choose our words carefully, but I'm amazed to learn how much of an impact our tone and body language have! Do we ever think about what our own posture communicates—our gestures, how we sit or stand, the look on our faces? And what about the impact of our tone of voice? Insights about message impact can help us make slight adjustments that increase our happiness because we enable more people to understand us.

Understanding can happily save us from hundreds of pointless arguments, emotional explosions, and relational breakdowns. People like to be understood.

Care for Others

The late Dr. Norman Vincent Peale asked an expert communicator for the reason behind his success in speaking in front of large audiences. The expert explained that an audience can almost immediately determine whether the one speaking really cares about them.[4] The same is true in our one-on-one conversations. Even when we are inept at communicating, if our talking shows interest in the other person, we will get a hearing.

As we've just learned, listeners pick up caring clues not only from our word selection, but from our actions, facial expressions, and tone of voice. I've seen people eager for strong friendships drive potential friends away by their mocking laughter, incessant talking, or unintended frowns—not realizing that they were giving a negative message of disregard for the other person. I think again of the one question that really helps me change negative messages into positive conversation: *How could I have said that better?*

Check yourself occasionally in the mirror to see if you are conveying yourself as being interested in people. Listen to the sound of your voice. Sort out in your mind the surface frustrations you might have with people's behavior and say what you intend to say to them as persons you value. When you cut others the same slack you would want from them, you convey that you care about them—with supportive words, a caring tone, a relaxed posture.

Emotional Control

Do you think it's possible to control emotions? A lot of friends and couples have separated because they lacked emotional control. "You make me mad! I'm out of here!" They assume that feelings such as anger, frustration, and jealousy just spontaneously enter their minds, determine their actions, and dictate their conversations. They say things like, "That's just the way I express myself. I can't change!" But you can! When feelings run high, you still can select your words and choose how you express them. As I'll describe in further detail in chapter nine, you can choose to take control of your emotions by choosing what you think.

Emotions are sometimes enormous, overwhelming, wild. We might even surprise ourselves by the intensity of our anger or sadness or exuberance. How can we learn to express such force in appropriate ways?

Most of us can sense when our emotions are beginning to rise. I have found that if I exert control soon enough, before the emotions become too intense, I can more easily control what I say and do. The longer I wait, the harder it is to respond objectively. My wife asked, "What if someone says something you don't like and instantly your emotions are at the boiling point?" I said, "Count to ten." Seriously. Counting to ten gives us time to get emotional control before saying words or taking actions that could destroy the relationship.

At times expressing strong emotions *is* appropriate. But the key to a sturdy relationship is to control the emotion so it works to improve the relationship—not destroy it. *Reason* (based on experience, research, and common sense) tells me that yelling, belittling, name-calling, and physical or verbal violence are weak reactions and counterproductive. *Willpower* is exercising my choice to control my emotions during the time to act. Like a jockey who, with a little bit on the tongue of a powerful horse, can guide a somewhat wild thoroughbred to the winner's circle, you too can rein in your emotions, choose to control your tongue, and win at contributing to a happy relationship.

Esteem of Your Self

Self-esteem is valuing the unique individual you are becoming. It does not mean that you think you are perfect or finished developing. Healthy self-esteem is not a sign of arrogance, but a sign of ego strength. In fact, without self-esteem, you are more likely to turn to others in desperate ways to feel good about yourself instead of building genuine relationships that nourish both participants.

Low self-esteem often results from accepting someone else's standard for your personal worth. But take a second look at that standard. Is it outer beauty, money, popularity, athletic skill? Is it fair or right to judge the value of human beings by these criteria? You can challenge standards of popular culture and choose to live up to standards of your own.

People who properly esteem themselves not only listen well but know when it's appropriate to talk. When they do talk, they don't need to dominate conversations, are not easily intimidated, and do not focus only on themselves.

Self-esteem enables you to affirm the value of others. When my son ran for senior class president in high school, I realized it was a teaching moment. I told him, "Jud, if you win, I will be proud of your effort. But if you lose, I will still be just as proud of you." I wanted my son to develop a healthy self-esteem regardless of external factors. Why? Persons with healthy esteem don't need to praise themselves. They concentrate on others and increase the happiness of mutual conversation.

Self-Confidence

Self-confident actions show inner self-esteem. *Self-esteem* is like the foundation for a building, and *self-confidence* is like the superstructure. Self-confidence is the part others see in the way we act and talk.

Suppose you are shy and don't experience self-confidence. What can you do then? Take these three actions:

1. Imagine what a *confident you* would say or do.
2. Picture the *positive results* that could follow confident action.
3. Choose to act *as if* you were confident.

Practice these three actions so that they become part of your interaction with people. When you practice confident actions, people know it and are more likely to listen to you. Self-confidence may cause you to take risks and sometimes fail, but when you fail, you can fail *forward*. You face yourself honestly, adjust your strategy, and try again.

I had a dream that illustrates these actions. At the time of the dream, I was in a doctoral program taught by an intimidating professor (large, belligerent, brilliant). One day he began to go around the circle of fifteen students in his class and seemed to delight in reducing each one to putty in his hands. I knew he was going to attack me the next day.

The night before my interrogation, I dreamt that the president of the United States invited me to discuss the issues of the day with him. My dream then took two different paths. The first path I replied, "Oh, no! I could never do that! I would not have anything to say." I felt miserable. Then my dream took me down a second path where I responded, "Oh, yes! Thank you! I would love to have this opportunity!" Whereas the first path (I'm too shy!) led to an unhappy failure, the second path (I'd love to!) led to an unforgettable experience that increased my confidence.

Like esteem of one's self, confidence is not built in a day. It takes a blueprint of who you want to become. It takes using the tools we have mentioned (attraction, listening, talking) to build the person who conveys confidence. People who are self-confident tend to win at what they do because they ask for advice, make plans, and move forward intentionally. Self-confidence causes people to want to respond to you in a positive way.

Sharing of One's Self

When it's appropriate, share your deeper thoughts and feelings with others to let them know who you are as a person. That sharing will be genuinely interesting to people who care. They will listen when you talk.

Knowing who to share ourselves with at a more personal level can be a bit risky because we don't know how others will respond, as Josh discovers.

> Josh: *You can tell me your dream.*
> Mia: *When I was a little girl I wanted to be a princes, you know, with a white dress, gold slippers, a big ballroom… But I guess that's kind of silly.*
> Josh: *Not at all. It's beautiful.*
> Mia: *What was your childhood dream, Josh?*
> Josh: *It's a secret. I've never told anyone this, but I wanted to be known as "Crazy Legs."*
> Mia: *Crazy Legs?*
> Josh: *Yeah, "Crazy Legs" was the nickname of a great football player who could run very fast, but he had skinny legs like mine.*
> Mia: *Crazy Legs! Hahaha! Wait 'til I tell the girls.*
> Josh: *Oh, no!*

Okay, Mia can't keep secrets. Maybe you too have been burned trying to express your deeper feelings. So how do we know when it's appropriate to share what's important to us? I find these questions help me know when it's suitable to share my more personal self.

- Is the person trustworthy?
- Has the person been truthful with me?

- Have I listened adequately to the person?
- Is the person asking for the information I could give?
- Will sharing my personal information strengthen the relationship?

If you answered no to any of these questions, it would be better to stay at a safer disclosure level. But consider this—if we assume too quickly that friends cannot be trusted, we close off an important part of ourselves. We even fail to discover the more interesting inner recesses of our own minds and hearts as well as that of others.

Author C. S. Lewis suggests in *The Great Divorce* that hell can be represented as people moving farther and farther away from each other until there is left only a vast wasteland.[5] Building strong friendships guards against feeling divorced from other people. Let's not lose the benefits of sharing ourselves with trustworthy friends.

In summary, you *can* talk so that others listen by using these principles of effective communication:

- Self-awareness—alertness to how you impact others.
- Understanding—interpreting and using words, tone, and posture winsomely.
- Care for others—being as interested in others as you are in yourself.
- Control of emotions—choosing how best to express feelings.
- Esteem of one's self—valuing the person you are becoming.

- Self-confidence—showing assurance in your own viewpoints.
- Sharing of one's self—trusting friends enough to confide your true self with them.

These principles help you talk in such a way that people want to listen to you. You feel affirmed as a person. You create friendships. Happiness increases.

PART TWO:
CONNECTING WELL

A friend sticks closer than a brother.

—Ancient Proverb

P eople close to you are sometimes better friends than blood
relatives are. They pick you up when you are down. They
upgrade the better part of your life.

Since emotional distance in relationships downgrades happiness,
Part Two focuses on relational tools that enable you to connect well
with relatives and friends by:

- Resolving conflicts
- Creating closeness
- Learning how to sustain relationships

These tools will help you fight against the forces that tear family
and friends apart and put together relationships that produce a deep
sense of well-being.

Connecting well creates more happiness.

RESOLVE CONFLICTS

Chapter 4

*Peace is not absence of conflict, it is the ability
to handle conflict by peaceful means.*

Ronald Reagan

t's a universal truth: everyone experiences conflict. You cannot be a family member or have a close friend for long without experiencing differences of opinion. Without resolution, bitterness can last a lifetime.

But conflicts are not really the problem! The problem is not even the number or frequency of conflicts. The problem is that sometimes we don't resolve them or we resolve them badly.

Some people assume peace means refusing to admit a conflict even exists. The story is told of two businessmen who got on the same elevator at the same time to go to their offices on the third and tenth floors, respectively. When the elevator reached the third floor, the first man turned to the second, spit in his face, and strode off the elevator. The second man never changed his demeanor, but simply took out his handkerchief and wiped his face dry. Dumbfounded, a passenger asked, "Why did you let him do that?" The man shook his head and said through clenched teeth, "I really don't care. It's his problem, not mine." I would not want to settle for that kind of feeble response. Nothing is resolved. What's to keep the third-floor businessman from spitting on his elevator companion again and again?

In this chapter I'll present a four-step model that will help you resolve disagreements. This tool disassembles a major barrier to happiness. Reconciliation becomes possible.

Why a Conflict-Resolution Model?

When emotions are intense, you don't have time to search your mind for an effective strategy. Models provide a ready, time-tested approach for resolution. I know that using any new model may seem uncomfortable at first, like learning to ride a bike. But after a few tries, it becomes second nature.

When you face on-going conflict with a friend or relative, I suggest taking four distinct steps and using their corresponding phrases to lessen conflict and generate closeness.[1]

Steps	Phrase for understanding
1. Define the problem.	"I hear you saying that…"
2. Look for agreement.	"Could we agree that…"
3. Understand feelings.	"I understand you might feel…"
4. State views calmly.	"I think…"

Let's look at each step in more detail.

Step 1. Define the Problem

Have you been in an argument only to discover that you're not sure what you are really arguing about? It happens. We get so involved in defending our position on some matter we forget what the other person might be trying to say.

> Alec: *I think we can ignore Dad's wishes that we donate a portion of our inheritance to charity and use it to pay some of my expenses instead.*
> Jennifer: *What? That's selfish! Don't you care what Dad intended?*

To reduce conflicts with your family or friends, clearly *define* any interpersonal problem that arises by getting to the root of the problem. Start the conversation by saying, "I hear you saying that..."

> Jennifer: *I hear you saying that you want to make sure your personal expenses are covered related to the disposition of Dad's will. Is that right?*
> Alec: *Yes! Since I'm without a job right now, I'm very concerned about my finances.*

As I mentioned in Chapter Two, use the tool of refusing to continue your discussion until you have stated your understanding of the problem to the other's satisfaction. You will be amazed at how this first step of defining the problem narrows the issue to a more manageable size.

To define problems, it helps to be aware of situations that may have caused them in the first place. Many different factors can cause us to react the way Jennifer did at first. Look at the following list of sources that tend to set people off on the wrong track in a conflict. Do you see any that seem especially relevant to you?

Causes of Discord

- Stress
- Tiredness
- Too many things to do
- Not enough money
- Clash of different beliefs
- A direct contradiction
- Lack of trust
- Harsh or accusing tone of voice
- Parents trying to control your affairs
- Coworker issues
- Overwhelming chores at home
- Feeling that you don't meet someone's standards
- Egocentricity
- Temperament
- Health concerns

Note: Sometimes defensiveness or refusing to look at the problem long enough to really define it is caused by *internal tensions*, not other people. If you wrestle with ongoing inner turmoil, you spend a lot of energy just trying to maintain or repair relationships. Maybe it's time to get help. Talk with a close friend or a counselor not just to air a grievance, but with a specific goal of finding a solution for your inner turmoil. Solve problems within by talking openly with conversational partners who will listen skillfully.

2. Look for Agreement

The second step in resolving conflict involves finding common ground. There must be something in your partner's viewpoint with which you can agree—some detail or obvious bit of truth. You will need to use your active listening skills in your search for something to agree on ... and that's part of its effectiveness. You are looking for areas of *agreement* because when you find common viewpoints, you cause the other person to relax. The conflict is now more manageable and a bit less threatening. Consequently your partner is encouraged to also calm down and the result is more openness to the other's viewpoint.

> Jennifer: *Could we agree on these points? You have critical financial issues. And we want to honor Dad's wishes if possible.*
> Alec: *I agree to that!*

"I agree..." messages limit the scope of your discussion. In this example, Jennifer didn't assume that Alec does not want to honor his father's wishes. And she uncovers the reasons behind Alec's statement. The problem is not solved, but its scope is more manageable. Looking for agreement reduces emotional distance and sets the stage for talking a conflict through to its resolution. Say *"Could we agree that..."* or *"I agree that..."* and then focus on details about which you and the other person can honestly agree. Here are additional examples:

- I agree that I said some unkind things. I'm sorry.
- I agree that I'm tired and may not be thinking clearly.
- I agree that your brother is thinking of our best interest.
- I agree that I mess up many times.

Searching for what you and your partner hold in common gives hope that the problem can be solved.

3. Understand Feelings

Business expert Stephen Covey said that the most important principle in interpersonal relations is this: "Seek first to understand, then be understood." When we understand feelings, we understand the person.

Few things are more important in a heated discussion than achieving true understanding. Say "I understand that you might feel…" and then complete this sentence with one word. Use a word that describes a *feeling*, not a thought or behavior. For example, you might use one of the following: Hurt / Anxious / Unsure of yourself / Afraid.

> Jennifer: *I understand that you might feel anxious about your loss of job and your finances. Is that right?*
> Alec: *Yes. And Dad's passing makes it all the harder because I'm afraid about my future. I'm not sure what I really want to happen here.*

You show that you *want* to understand by identifying the other's feelings. One word of caution: do not say, "I know exactly how you feel." It can backfire. The other person may retort, "No, you don't! You are not me!" To avoid the impression that you are minimizing the other person's feelings, it's important to ask, as Jennifer did, the follow-up question, "Is that right?" Then actively listen to the person's response. Your aim is to understand the other's true feeling, not to win the argument. You're not playing a game where the goal is to win. If you're trying to connect well, "losing" the argument may mean that you win the friendship.

When your goal is to understand the other's feelings, the result is powerfully positive because most people desperately want to be understood. In fact, not understanding the other's feelings may be the real cause of the argument! Discovering what your partner is feeling helps resolve conflict.

4. State Your Views Calmly

If understanding each other's feelings does not solve the problem, then state your views as calmly and briefly as possible. You can say, "I think…" or "The way I see it is…"

> Jennifer: *I think the bequest Dad left us is very generous and more than covers our expenses. I think we can still give something to charity. Do you agree?*
>
> Alec: *I see your point. Dad's bequest will certainly help! I guess I was so focused on my expenses that I didn't think about charity. Let's honor Dad's request, even if I have to use some of the bequest money to get by right now.*

When you have defined the real problem, agreed on a few key points, accurately identified the feelings being expressed, then you can make your point calmly. Calmness helps the other person listen better because he doesn't have to be defensive. For example:

- The way I see it is that we had a prior agreement.
- I think there are at least two ways to view this matter.
- I think that I need some peace and quiet when I come home from work.
- I think that my work must come first; recreation comes after that.

Make every effort to avoid name-calling, put-downs, and judgmental evaluations. Raising your voice is a useless reaction to the tensions of the moment. Choose to speak firmly without speaking loudly. Choose to eliminate threatening talk because although threats might "win" the argument temporarily, threats fail to bring the resolution you want.

In the midst of discord, individuals often speak *at* each other, missing each other's points and generating more heat than light. Resolving conflicts can produce dramatic changes in your relationships. With the conflict resolution model, the focus of the controversy gradually changes from attacking one another to attacking a mutual problem and solving it.

As the shift in focus occurs, there is a corresponding change in the nature of your relationship. You speak *with*, not *at* the other. You are less defensive and more open. You generate less anger and achieve greater understanding. You are happier!

Applying the Conflict-Resolution Model

Let's apply the four steps to another example by comparing responses that produce discord with responses that generate resolution. We'll look at an area of common discord between husband and wife—finances.

Say a husband bursts into the house waving a checkbook and shouting: "Hey, we're overdrawn again! You forgot to record a check! Maybe you like paying overdraft fines! How irresponsible can you get?"

Discord Exchange

Wife: I'm not the only one who doesn't balance the checkbook!

Husband: But you always mess up when our balance is very low.

Wife: Okay, Perfect One. Do you remember the last time we had to pay a fine? It was because you were speeding. $75 bucks!

Husband: What about the time you hit the side of the garage with the car? $785 bucks down the drain!

Resolution Exchange

Wife: <u>I hear</u> you saying that you're upset because I forgot to record a check.

Husband: Yes! What were you thinking?

Wife: <u>I agree</u> that it is hard for us to save. Everything costs so much. We certainly don't need extra expenses like fines.

Husband: I'm afraid we're not going to have the money we need for our new boat.

Wife: <u>I understand</u> that you might be really frustrated. Right?

Husband: Yup.

Wife: <u>I think</u> I really messed up. I'm very sorry. Will you forgive me?

The Discord Exchange shows a conflict that just got worse; the real cause of tension is lost in mutual recriminations. The Resolution

Exchange uncovered a major frustration in the husband. His initial outburst was triggered only incidentally by the overdraft fine. Now that the real concern has been brought out into the open, the husband and wife are on the right path to solve the problem together.

Does a Resolution Exchange always work this well? No. There are too many human variables involved. But if in our talking and listening we use this conflict resolution model to increase our understanding of each other, we are doing our part to lessen conflict and build happier relationships.

CREATE CLOSENESS

Chapter 5

*Affection is responsible for nine-tenths of what-
ever solid and durable happiness there is in our
lives.*

—C. S. Lewis

Susan and Michael had few conflicts in their marriage. They didn't argue, yell, or get upset. Yet something was missing—a feeling of togetherness and the solid happiness of mutual affection. They yearned to create closeness, but they didn't know how.

Bree, Adrianna, and Ann were in the same social circle. Although they wanted to share their deeper thoughts and feelings as friends, they never seemed to go beyond superficial chatter due to mistrust, not enough time, fear of judgment.

Interpersonal closeness is not easy or automatic, but it's worth it. You and I need to build relationships with the right tools if we want to create acceptance and repair misunderstanding. In this chapter, we focus on four powerful principles that can help you produce relational closeness. When you practice them, you feel better connected with others. You multiply each other's happiness.

Forgiveness

What breaks the connection between husband and wife, parents and children, and those who have been friends? Sometimes it's hurt feelings, a harsh tone of voice, a misunderstanding, a desire for revenge, a touch of meanness. One powerful tool that repairs broken relationships is forgiveness for actual or perceived wrongs.

Nothing brings people together and restores wounded hearts like forgiveness. Dr. Martin Luther King Jr. declared, "We must develop and maintain the capacity to forgive. He who is devoid of the power to forgive is devoid of the power to love."[1]

To stress the importance of forgiveness, Jesus elaborated on this part of the famous Lord's Prayer: "For if you forgive others their trespasses, your Heavenly Father will also forgive you, but if you do not forgive others their trespasses, neither will your Father forgive your trespasses."[2]

What about forgiving only when we feel like it or when the other person apologizes? Not an option. If we want the benefits of forgiveness, we need to initiate forgiveness.

To forgive whether you feel like it or not really is a smart thing to do because it almost always creates closeness. In fact, I think one of the reasons God commands that we forgive others is to prevent a downward spiral of repelling each other—hurts leading to resentments leading to conflicts leading to relational distance. Distance causes us to misunderstand, mistrust, and mistake the motives of someone even as close as a spouse. Forgiveness, on the other hand, benefits the forgiver as much as it does the one being forgiven. With forgiveness, closeness is possible.

If forgiveness yields such benefits, why are we not quicker to say, "I'm sorry. Will you forgive me?" Perhaps we think apologizing is a sign of weakness. But consider this: to the person who has been wronged, an apology often comes through as *a sign of strength*. Why? Requesting forgiveness suggests a willingness to face the situation, to admit wrong, and to take responsibility for bridging the relational gap caused by the hurt. No puny person can do it.

What if you're ready to forgive, but your spouse or friend continues to defend his or her actions? You can control only your own actions, but you can provide the best environment for an apology by taking these steps:

First, a*void a blame mentality*—a pattern of blaming the other person for the problem. Such a mentality actually focuses on *me* rather than *we*. Defending one's self and accusing the other person appears to be more important than building relationship. It doesn't motivate closeness. It puts your ego above deepening your relationship with the other person.

Second, *be willing to initiate the healing process by saying "I'm sorry."* Follow that with asking the greatest healing question: "Will you forgive me for my contribution to the problem?" Superficial apologies do not fool anyone for long. But genuine regret for mistakes actually strengthens trust.

Third, *support your words with actions*. A verbal acknowledgement of wrong needs to be followed by a hug, an accepting look, a willingness to listen to more of the hurt if necessary—these actions underline your words. They communicate that you genuinely value the other person and consider the friendship worth building.

Forgiveness can turn even "emotional strangers" into companions because it decreases the desire for revenge. It bridges psychological distance by putting uncomfortable feelings into words that heal rather than hurt.

An added benefit is that forgiveness has a transforming effect on you as well as a family member or friend. You might be surprised at how good it feels and how quickly it can fuel warmth in a relationship. Relational distance a mile wide can be reduced to nothing in a second. With the regular practice of forgiveness, you feel free of guilt. Your relationship flourishes. You're energized. You're happy.

Trust

In *The Speed of Trust,* Steven M. R. Covey asserts that trust impacts relationships 24/7, 365 days a year: "It undergirds and affects the quality of every relationship, every communication, every effort in which we are engaged. It changes the quality of every moment and alters the trajectory of every future outcome of our lives."[3]

Trust in relationships refers to letting others into our "bubble"— our personal space. In trusting family relationships, Mom is not afraid to speak her understanding of truth in love. Dad is strong enough to show emotion at times and not to put up a façade of always being right. Children can express how they feel without being defensive or angry. Within tight family circles, each trusts the other to know what's within his or her mind and heart. This kind of trust makes relationships stronger and more satisfying.

We soon learn that as beneficial as trust is, it does not come easily, even within families. Why? The ancient Hebrew Scriptures tell of humankind's fall into a state of broken and difficult relationships, a story that resonates with most of us.[4]

Trust between spouses, parents and children, and close friends is damaged by this brokenness and selfish pride—a desire to make ourselves look good at the expense of someone else. Self-seeking pride drives people apart. Has that been your experience?

FINDING HAPPINESS

When I hesitate to share important thoughts and feelings, it's usually because I don't trust the other person with the information. I ask myself, *Will he understand what I mean? Will she keep my private business in confidence?* Often we don't know the answers for certain. The temptation is to give up trying because trust is risky. And some individuals don't deserve our full trust. But as a friend or family member tries to earn our confidence, we need to be willing to trust at appropriate levels.

It's normal for humans to get suspicious or anxious at times. Maybe we've had trust backfire. Our best intentions in expressing trust sometimes get sidetracked. How do we keep from destroying what closeness we have worked hard to build? The answer revolves around the next personal characteristic that fuels closeness.

Restraint

Restraint refers to the ability to control impulses. Where our normal tendency might be to vent anger, we can restrain that tendency by channeling anger into a useful purpose. For example, we can choose to say constructive instead of destructive words. Our ability to restrain tendencies is one of the qualities that sets us apart from animals. It's a key component in creating closeness.

An ancient proverb made this comparison: "Better a patient man than a warrior, a man who controls his temper than one who takes a city."[5] Perhaps the greater power of patience is needed most in our tendency to express every feeling that surfaces. Let's look at the following responses typical in some marriages. In these conflicts, which response reflects your usual reaction?

55

Hair left in the sink

(A) Honey, I love your hair—but not when it's in the sink.
(B) Hey Pig Pen! You did it again! Can't you learn to clean up after yourself?

Snoring in the night

(A) Shut up! You sound like a Harley! I can't sleep!
(B) George, you're snoring! Please blow your nose and roll over on your side.

Late for an appointment

(A) Aren't you ready yet? You can't change what nature's given you. No one's going to look at you anyway! Let's go!
(B) Hey, the meeting starts at eight. I'd really like to get there on time. Can you be ready to leave at 7:15 as we agreed?

A public school teacher took a course on closeness that my wife and I were teaching. After hearing about the advantages provided by restraint, she wrote:

> I have a terrible time switching roles from school to home. At work I take charge, I teach, I delegate, I discipline, I supervise. When I come home, that role doesn't work. I often forget to change hats. But I'm learning. Although I've been practicing restraint for some years, I sometimes revert to being a "Little General" at home. I really don't want to be that way with my husband even though it comes so natural for me. When I work at restraining myself, I find his leadership refreshing.[6]

One area where we need to exercise restraint is in talking *too* much. Of course, some have to deal with a tendency to not talk much at all! So how do we find a proper balance? I find the "50-50 rule" helps: to listen at least as much as I talk. Take the initiative in making communication mutually satisfying by applying the 50-50 rule. Ask questions. Resist the urge to talk too much because you value long-term closeness more than the momentary rush of telling your own story.

A proverb reminds us that discernment is sometimes best served by silence: "A person who lacks judgment derides his neighbor, but an understanding person holds his tongue."[7]

Occasionally *understanding* means you don't say anything. You "hold your tongue." In my marriage, Janiece sometimes softly responds to a difference in our temperaments and ways of doing things with an "Oh, well." Then we laugh or smile that we still can be so different after years of togetherness.

To create closeness, our aim is to major in topics of importance. The important question we ask ourselves is, *Will my talking help to strengthen this relationship?* If not, we listen actively. We know our time to talk will come. Restraint is a conscious decision to refuse the impulse to just say something. It gives us that split second to adjust what we say or how we say something so that we communicate in a way that creates closeness.

Encouragement

Do you ever wish some family member or friend would say to you, "Good job! I knew you could do it." or "I love that idea. It's got great possibilities!" When you hear those words, you feel encouraged to continue.

Whether discouragement results from setting unrealistic goals or put-downs from those around us, discouragement hurts. We live in a world that constantly reminds us of our limitations and imperfections. We may not make as much money as our neighbor, or look as healthy, or receive adequate attention for our work, or have a fine house. We face the assessments of final exams, qualifying tests, and performance reviews. Some of the time we do not measure up to someone's standards, or even our own. Negative social pressure can make us feel worthless. It can deplete self-esteem.

When you encourage your family member or close friend, you call forward his or her courage. You help that person feel bold enough to face life's challenges. In his letter to the Thessalonians, the apostle Paul urged his readers to take cheering on the other person as part of their purpose in life: "Encourage one another and build each other up."[8]

What encourages you? I find that unconditional acceptance and words of affirmation work marvelously to lift my spirit and help me to encourage others I meet. A proverb pictures an encouraging word as giving life that branches outward: "A soothing tongue is a tree of life."[9]

Some key "tree of life" phrases that build people up and draw them close are collected in a book by successful businessman Rich DeVos called *Ten Powerful Phrases for Positive People.*

1. I'm wrong.
2. I'm sorry.
3. You can do it.
4. I believe in you.
5. I'm proud of you.
6. Thank you.

7. I need you.
8. I trust you.
9. I respect you.
10. I love you.[10]

When used sincerely, these phrases have a potent effect. Not sure? Think about how you feel when someone says any of these phrases to you.

What encourages us likely will encourage close friends. Here are additional examples of words that build up:

- You have a wonderful, outgoing personality. Let's not compare ourselves to anybody. You are the one I want to be with.
- I believe you will win with this project. But if you don't, you're still a winner with me.
- We're in this together, no matter what happens.
- I like the fun times we have together.
- Give it your best. I'm cheering for you.

In summary, these four values are like anchors for your relationship:

- Forgiveness
- Trust
- Restraint
- Encouragement

They hold the relationship secure even in difficult times.

Decide where you may be a bit weak in using these values. Choose to do your part in creating closeness and connecting well with friends and family. Happiness is at stake!

SUSTAIN FRIENDSHIPS

Chapter 6

Friendship is unnecessary, like philosophy, like art...
It has no survival value; rather it is one of those
things that gives value to survival.

—C. S. Lewis

Y ou've seen it happen—relationships that last through difficult times. What kept these relationships strong? It seems counterintuitive in our culture for people to stay together, whether in marriage or friendship. But in Chapter Four, you gained tools to resolve conflict and create closeness. Now you and I need tools that keep friends and family close ... and add value to survival.

Sustaining friendships has been hard for me. Before I was twenty-five, I had lived in nineteen places. It's difficult to keep any relationship going when you move all the time. But I did learn the enduring value of commitment.

Genuine friendships depend on robust commitment—the willingness to sacrifice one's own desires to attain a greater good. Thomas Bradbury, psychologist at the UCLA Relationship Center, describes why commitment is necessary:

When the stakes are high, our relationships are vulnerable. When we're under a great deal of stress or when there is a high-stakes decision on which you disagree, those are defining moments in a relationship. What our data indicate is that committing to the relationship rather than committing to your own agenda and your own immediate needs is a far better strategy. We're not saying it's easy.[1]

Commitment guides our behavior so it's consistent with what we value. Although sustaining friendships requires a similar commitment from the other person, we can enhance our part by consciously choosing to commit to the following relational principles so that people who matter to us count us as friends.[2]

Commitments That Sustain Friendship

As you consider commitments you choose to make, put a check by those actions you want to fortify first.

1. *I want to be a friend.* List in the margin all the qualities you want in a friend. Then ask yourself which of those qualities you have or need to develop further. Commit yourself to improving those qualities.

2. *I will consciously make the satisfaction, security, and development of my friend as significant to me as my own.* This commitment is an adaptation of psychologist Harry Stack Sullivan's classic definition of love or affection.[3] Acting on this principle destroys barriers between people and builds a closeness that generates a delightful sense of connection.

3. *I will make adequate time for friendship.* If you would like an acquaintance to be one of your best friends, you will need to spend time together. Where will you find the time? Ask yourself, "Can I

reduce time I spend on social media or the Internet in order to spend more face time with close friends?" Friends need time together to develop mutual understanding. Emotions need time to become clear and expressed. Thoughts need time to be collected, sifted, organized, and articulated.

4. *I will enjoy the uniqueness of my friend.* True friends affirm each other's distinctiveness in contrast to our common tendency to want to duplicate ourselves. We see our friends not as copies of ourselves, but as complements who add to rather than detract from our own identity. If you want to build strong friendships, do three things consistently: a) allow for habits and temperaments unlike your own, b) cut the other some slack, and c) choose to see differences as a challenge to your skill at achieving cooperation.

5. *I will avoid criticizing, condemning, and judging my friends.* This commitment is so huge that it's worth writing on a sticky note and putting it on your mirror as a daily reminder. It's sensible because none of us is perfect and it's necessary because our viewpoints and actions aren't always right nor others' always wrong. Check your body signals, tone of voice, and words. Do they convey judgment or acceptance? Supporting the person while objecting to the behavior provides the best chance of maintaining friendship and motivating change.

6. *I will look for opportunities to give sincere compliments.* The "law of mutual exchange" works in a positive way when we give compliments that draw out the best in each other. Others are motivated to look for the best in us. Compliments such as the following decrease emotional distance.

- I like the way you care for yourself.
- Your views on this topic show sensitivity to nuance.
- You put a lot of good thinking into this project. It shows.
- You seem to know just when to say the right thing.
- Your friendship means a great deal to me. You make me so happy.

7. I will try to understand a friend's feelings. I remember when a trusted friend made time in his schedule to sit down and listen to what I was feeling. It made a huge difference in my own sense of well-being. Can you be that kind of person to your friend?

8. I will focus my attention on the other person. To understand your friend is to appreciate your friend's perspective, even if it's different from your own. It means you listen at least as much as you talk. Commitment to listening and asking questions for clarity closes the gap between two people. The better we understand, the greater the opportunity for acceptance and appreciation, which are building blocks for a sustainable friendship.

9. I will fight for closeness. When most disagreements occur, the pattern is familiar: two different worlds of thought and feeling colliding, then an explosion of hostile words or actions, followed by hurt feelings and psychological distance. You can choose to model a different style of disagreement. As discussed in chapter 4, a conflict-resolution model gives you the opportunity to pursue greater closeness instead of destroying your relational bridge. Because it's possible to "fight" in a way both participants win, I want to stress again these simple rules of good interpersonal relationships:

- I will not yell, insult, lie, or call the other names.
- I will repeat the other's feelings *to that person's satisfaction* before presenting my own point. For example, "You think I don't care about your folks. Is that right?"
- I will try to understand my friend instead of dominating the conversation.

What a difference these three simple habits could make in our disagreements! Of course, there still might be hurt feelings, defensiveness, insecurity, anger, and a need to change behavior. But consider the benefits: the really damaging punches would be eliminated; getting on the same page would supersede one-upmanship; listening carefully would dominate. How could anyone lose this kind of fight?

10. *I will ask the greatest healing question.* Earlier in the book, I mentioned one question, when asked in sincerity, produces remarkable healing in relationships: "Will you forgive me for my contribution to the problem?" It's worth writing it down and committing it to memory. Notice that by asking this question, you are not assuming all the blame or passing on the blame. In fact, you are not trying to assess who is most at fault or who is "right" and who is "wrong"—all dead-end objectives. You are simply acknowledging that you contributed *something* (even though it might be only 5 percent) to the problem: a judgmental tone of voice, an unfair criticism, bringing up a negative action from the past. But if you want healing, percentages of blame do not matter. You can say, "I'm sorry for my contribution to this problem. Will you forgive me?" When I honestly ask this question, I find that mountains of bitterness disappear. Miles of psychological distance vanish. Wow!

The Happiness of Enduring Friendships

Gretchen Rubin, author of *The Happiness Project,* declares in one of her blogs:

> *You need close, long-term relationships; you need to be able to confide in others; you need to belong; you need to get and give support. Studies show that if you have five or more friends with whom to discuss an important matter you're far more likely to describe yourself as "very happy."*[4]

When happy friendships develop, what do they look like? Here's my experience: each partner is willing to talk freely and listen deeply. Even small, insignificant bits of information are received without judgment. Respect, self-worth, and positive perspectives blossom.

Commitments in friendship result in a greater experience of stability and well-being. When you actually look for ways to enrich the lives of friends, your own life is enhanced. You feel motivated to step out of the coldness of impersonal thoughts and into the warmth (and fun) of your thoughts coming alongside another's, adding to a sense of togetherness. Commitments that anchor friendship yield happiness.

PART THREE:
LIVING WITH PURPOSE

If you board the wrong train, it is no use running along the corridor in the other direction.

— Dietrich Bonhoeffer

uilding Friendships (Part One) and Connecting Well (Part Two) ignite happiness because you *receive in* from others both information and experience that gives value to life.

Living with Purpose (Part Three) enables you to use your interpersonal skills to take two purposeful actions:

- *give back*—passing on your knowledge to someone who can learn from it, and
- *move forward*—crafting a life purpose statement that energizes you.

Life is like a labyrinth—so many paths available, so many ways to mess up. Where is the path that leads to a happy destination? We have noted that self-absorption is dead-end. It fails to satisfy. The path of an other-centered focus helps you find happiness.

Living with purpose helps you board the right train and move in the right direction.

MENTOR OTHERS

Chapter 7

*Remember that mentor leadership is all about
serving.*

—Coach Tony Dungy

Serving multiplies happiness—the other person's happiness
as well as your own! Do you remember times you've helped
someone learn something or take an action they thought impossible?
Can you picture the faces of those you helped gain new insights?
Were those faces smiling? How about yours?

You can probably recall life-changing advice that a teacher, parent,
or coach gave you that helped you launch out in a new direction. Are
you interested in passing on lessons you have learned to someone
less experienced? As a mentor, you might not be able to help very
much. But the help you give could be like a rudder on a ship—a little
gizmo producing significant change.

I faced a mentor opportunity with my son when toward the end of
his junior year in high school, Judson began to think intensely about
his future. Crucial decisions lay before him that would affect his life

for years to come. With so little knowledge, he wanted to know from people with more experience how to avoid huge mistakes.

If you are skillful in helping youth, you can make a major impact. You can help them ask the right questions and enable them to take actions that matter most to them. You can teach them some basics of decision-making. You can support them as they sort out their confusion. You can listen and encourage. The difference you make can be profound.

Since youth need to establish their own identities, we need to listen much and ask questions that help them reach their destination. Opportunities come at unexpected times—when your brother or sister laments, "I don't know what I want to do with my life!" or the person you are mentoring says, "Should I go directly into the Marines or go to college?" how will you respond?

This chapter helps prepare you for four important questions youth ask about their future. For each question, we'll look at basic concepts to keep in mind, key values to communicate, and some door-opening strategies for starting healthy discussion. It may have been years since you really examined the foundation for what you think and do, but when you are willing to identify again your own inner core of values, you benefit as well as the one you mentor.

Education—"What Do I Want to Learn?"

During the summer before their senior high school years, our two children, Judson and Jessica, received a host of brochures advertising particular colleges or fields of study. It set the stage for great soul-searching. They began to think: *This is a big deal. I'm growing up. I must decide what I'm going to do with my life. What kind of training do*

I want? Help! Your brothers or sisters or children or coworkers also might be asking for help.

Educational Facts to Consider

To gather facts about further education, ask yourself these questions:

- *Is my protégé (the person I lead) ready for college?* People mature at different rates. Although schools group children according to age as a matter of convenience, graduating from high school doesn't necessarily mean that teens are mentally or emotionally ready for college.

- *Should my protégé go to college?* There's no automatic answer. Not every youth should go to college, even if mentally capable of succeeding at that level of education. A technical school or a first job may be more in line with your protégé's needs and aspirations. If you try to persuade him to go to college when he feels it's not right for him, you may cause him to feel guilty, rebellious, or inadequate.

- *Which colleges best fit my protégé?* Vast differences exist regarding academic standards and educational theories. Do you know what a school values … and do you support those values? Does the college place a higher priority on athletics or academic excellence? Is there a balance?

- *What do I have to offer?* Although you play an important part in helping youth make decisions, it is not helpful if in your counsel, you're trying to relive your own college dreams. Are you really seeking *their* welfare? Do you encourage the study and reading habits they'll need for higher education? If college is not an option, can you point them to where they will get the life skills they need, such as correspondence schools, continuing education seminars, or night and weekend classes?

- *What resources does my protégé have?* The cost of a college education is significant. How will your youth's education be funded? Have you advised him or her adequately to explore scholarship aid? If not, do you know where to suggest they go for more information?

Making a list of the questions you need to answer and searching the internet or your library for answers is a helpful way to prepare yourself for mentoring.

Educational Values to Share

List the values that have steadied you, anchored you in turbulent times, and that you want to transfer to your protégé. The following list will get you started.

- *Learning is enjoyable.* A positive attitude about learning new information makes grappling with even difficult concepts rewarding. Encourage your protégé to approach reading, courses, and discussions with the attitude that they can benefit from learning the subject.
- *Education never ends.* By your own example, you can convey that a teachable spirit looks for ways to gain knowledge and search for truth.
- *Gaining wisdom is a lifetime goal.* Youth may not realize knowledge and wisdom are *not* the same. I counseled a brilliant doctor with vast knowledge who made really dumb mistakes in her interpersonal relationships. In spite of all

she knew, she was not wise. Wisdom—learning how to best use knowledge—equips us for living an abundant life.

- *"Dig deep, irrigate widely."* A favorite slogan of Dr. Ken Pike, former head of the Linguistics Department at the University of Michigan, the image suggests a value I want to convey to the youth I lead: thinking well may be difficult, but the deeper we go, the broader and more useful the application.

- *Reason and faith are complimentary.* Scientific process is built on the belief that certain natural laws will continue to hold true, whether or not they are fully understood. Water always boils at 212 degrees at sea level. Gravity always pulls objects heavier than air to the ground. Without faith in natural laws, reason and science would be impossible. Likewise, faith in God, who is far more mysterious than any natural law, is not contrary to reason or science.

- *Wisdom requires diligent searching.* Discerning the best option takes effort. King Solomon mentored his son to earnestly search for true wisdom.

  My son, if you accept my words ... turning your ear to wisdom and applying your heart to understanding, and if you call out for insight and cry aloud for understanding, and if you look for it as for silver and search for it as for hidden treasure, then you will understand the fear of the Lord and find the knowledge of God.[1]

Educational Questions to Ask

To encourage youth to make good decisions, make a habit of asking good questions. Granted, a lot of values are "caught instead of taught." But one way to "catch values" is to help your protégé develop an inquiring mind. As you ask questions, listen actively to your protégé's thoughts. Here are a few ways to get the discussion going.

- Ask for their opinion about news in your community, nation, and the world.
- Raise questions from your reading material. When something interests you, talk about it. It may encourage your protégé to read more if they see you benefit from your reading.
- Create an atmosphere where it feels safe for youth to express even half-formed ideas. Instead of an argument, aim for a mutual exchange of ideas. Never ridicule—it rarely works positively. Invite your protégés' views on topics of interest to them.
- If you sense resistance, ask if your thoughts about education make sense. Your credibility increases when you admit mistakes of logic or reason. You can say, "I guess that doesn't make a whole lot of sense, does it?" "Well, I think you are right; I was wrong." Honesty plus humility helps generate credibility.
- Ask questions or make comments that expand your protégés' ability to explain their thoughts. Encourage new insights or logical connections:
  - "I think you made an excellent point!"
  - "That sounds interesting."
  - "Can you tell me more?"
  - "Have you thought about what you would do if…?"
  - "How did you arrive at that conclusion?" "Then what?"

You want them to think deeply and feel comfortable stating their thoughts.

Vocation—"What Will I Do With My Life?"

In one of our "heart-to-heart" talks, my son Jud said, "Dad, I don't know what kind of work I should do. I think about it and try to weigh all the factors. Sometimes I want to know so badly that it hurts, like a pain right here in my chest."

Youth probably think a lot more about their future than we realize. They have to experience much of the thinking, and the hurting, themselves. Yet, at some point we may have gone through the same process. Perhaps we still wonder whether we made the right decision. If we have recently changed to a new line of work, we may understand some of their pressures. Examining our own experience helps us respond when teens ask, "What will I do with my life? How do I decide? What factors should I consider?"

Vocational Facts to Consider

- Choosing a career without giving it much thought can produce long-term unhappiness. Management experts estimate that nearly 80 percent of all Americans are dissatisfied with their work. Surveys have shown that many associate work with apathy, boredom, nervousness, shouting matches, and daily humiliation.
- Most high school students do not have realistic expectations about their careers according to the National Assessment of Educational Progress.
- People skills—being able to relate well—rather than technical skills top the list of what's needed for promotion in both technical and professional vocations.

- Work that draws upon one's interests, skills, and training can be immensely satisfying and rewarding.
- Overwork can be counterproductive. Surveys conducted by the Institute for Social Research at the University of Michigan suggest that long hours of part-time work by high school students are linked with weak school performance, low college aspirations, and higher drug use.

Vocational Values to Share

Vocational values help clear away the fog that surrounds a multitude of career choices. They make clear the path that leads to satisfying results. You may need to dig deeply into your own supply of values to mentor well. Here are some of my work values that may stimulate the development of your own.

- Happiness at work often results when people use their natural abilities.
- A sense of mission or "rightness" about a particular work can lift it out of meaningless routine.
- Aiming for excellence in work creates a sense of satisfaction and confidence.
- Working too long almost always causes stress, fatigue, impatience, and neglect of important relationships.
- Learning negotiation skills is valuable in every line of work.

Vocational Questions to Ask

Let us keep in mind that the decision process for youth may lead to dead ends, false starts, and impulse answers. It can be messy. That's why when you mentor youth, you provide the balance they need between stability and the risk of a new venture. You help youth when you ask questions like the following.

- What kinds of activities do you feel you are good at?
- What kind of people would you enjoy working with—thinkers, practitioners, craftsmen, decision makers, leaders, or a combination?
- What area of the country would you want to settle in—near or far away from home?
- What kind of work would you aspire to—administration, service related, research, data entry, public relations, work with your hands?
- What would make you feel good about yourself—excellent work habits, public approval, promotions, working by yourself, directing a team?

Avoid interrogating or judging youth. These questions require time for reflection and sensitivity on your part. Ask when would be the right time to listen to their ideas about future work. Think of their answers as ideas in the process of becoming clear rather than their final decisions. You might want to come back later to a thought and check its progress.

Adults kill enthusiasm by overreacting when a younger person's ideas seem senseless or impossible. Judgmental statements sap energy and drive: "You couldn't get a job in that field" or "You couldn't stand the pressure." If you've already given an insulting response, you can recover by saying, "Remember when I said `You couldn't stand the pressure'? This is what I wish I had asked, `How do you think you would handle the pressures that come with that work?'"

Testing vocational interest and aptitude can reveal new possibilities or confirm hunches. But actual experience on a variety of jobs provokes fresh insights. Arrange for your protégé to ask business owners or workers questions like these:

- What is a typical workday like for you?
- Why did you choose your line of work?
- If you could make your decision again, what would you do differently?
- What are some problems you deal with at work?
- What do you like and dislike about your work?

Talk openly about your own work—what disappoints and what satisfies. If possible, ask the person you mentor if he or she would like to work with you for a day. Arrange for them to do activities that would help them understand the nature of your work.

Imagine the value of this approach to vocation. Do you see how it might have helped you in your own career choice? Taking the time to mentor youth along the best path suited for them could make a huge difference in the course of their lives. A vocation that fits their interests and abilities could be key to their happiness at work.

Money—"What Are My Priorities?"

A journalist tells a story about a man at a car rental counter who angrily insisted he needed a black Continental because everyone going to his New Year's Eve party would be driving black Continentals. On the man's tee shirt was this inscription: "The one who dies with the most toys wins." Did the man really believe that motto? Is it an adequate philosophy for life? Did anyone help him when he was a young man to discern what his priorities would be?

Money Facts to Consider

Since facts about money habits and statistics will change, it is well to check leading economic indicators for current patterns. At the present time, here are some sobering trends in the US worth considering:

- Over 50 percent of US families spend more than they earn.
- Average Americans incur about $15,950 in credit card debt. If you make a $360 payment every month at an annual APR of 15 percent, it would take about thirty years to pay off this debt.
- On his website, financial expert Dave Ramsey shows how it's possible to live debt-free.

Money Values to Share

- Money is morally neutral; it's neither good nor bad. It can be used by individuals for great benefit or terrible destruction.
- Affluence can be a source of personal happiness, *and* it can make a positive difference in society.[2]
- Due to preconceived biases, people critical of wealth may refuse to see that money can be used for great social good. Similarly, wealthy people may not have considered how their money could help others less fortunate.
- Simply *giving* money to persons or organizations may do more harm than good if it promotes laziness or an "entitlement mentality" that reduces initiative and gratitude.

- Money can deceive us into thinking we are totally self-sufficient. It is when we feel gratitude for material blessings that happiness increases.
- Economic setbacks like unemployment can signal a big decline in happiness, *or* it can lead to rethinking one's values in life. Wise counsel can help individuals reset their course in life according to their core values.

Money Questions to Ask

1. What are your income goals? What matters to you financially?
2. How do your goals fit in with your sense of purpose in life?
3. How would you prioritize your goals?
4. By age forty or fifty, what amount of income would you like to receive?
5. How do you plan to manage your money (instead of letting your money managing you)?

Your questions will take on greater credibility if you ask and answer them first yourself. Remember that more money does not always satisfy. Perhaps we all can learn from businessman Lee Atwater's change of perspective:

> I acquired more wealth, power, and prestige than most. But you can acquire all you want and still feel empty. What power wouldn't I trade for a little more time with my family? What price wouldn't I pay for an evening with friends? It took a deadly illness to put me eye-to-eye with that truth—a truth that the country, caught up in its ruthless ambitions and moral decay, can learn on my dime.[3]

Let's face it: money can deceive us. We might assume we are doing "good" (helping make the world a better place) when we are only doing "well" (accumulating enough toys to "win" social approval). Without compassionate generosity, evidence suggests that money can destroy our sense of well-being. But with compassion that appropriately provides for people less fortunate, we can experience a deep satisfaction. The happy smiles of the recipients of wise benevolence multiply our own happiness.

Marriage—"Who Will I Marry?"

Your protégé might not be married yet, but likely wants to be someday. Most youth wonder with whom they will spend their lives. They ask, "How will I know if I really *love* somebody?"

Psychiatrist Harry Stack Sullivan provides a definition of love, mentioned in Chapter 6, that can serve as a benchmark for answering this question. He says, "A state of love exists when the satisfaction and security of the other person becomes as significant to you as your own satisfaction and security."[4]

I like this definition because it provides an ongoing personal metric for gauging a love relationship. In some ways it appears to be countercultural to what is called a "Me, Me, Me" generation. But sincere love for the other person coupled with concern for his or her satisfaction and security is necessary for personal happiness. Lena Dunham (one who appears to understand contemporary culture and is a two-time winner of Golden Globes), has her TV character comment on her two-day experience in a loving family relationship, "What I didn't realize is that I was lonely in such a deep, deep way. I want what everyone wants, to be happy."[5]

Mentors and parents likely would agree that Sullivan's definition of love is relevant today because they understand that if love is to be long-lasting, it requires that individuals actively seek the satisfaction and security of the other person. It is that security that provides a foundation for personal growth, for self-expansion, for happiness.

Happy marriages are based on a love commitment rather than feelings because, although powerful, feelings are temporary. Beauty fades. Hormones quiet down. According to many studies and hundreds of my own counseling cases, it appears clear that sustainable happiness in marriage requires a love commitment described by Sullivan.

Marriage Facts to Consider

Young adults need to understand some basic relational truths so that they can enter a relationship with their eyes wide open.

- The U.S. Census Bureau records that around 50 percent of marriages in the United States and other developed nations end in divorce.
- In a 2012 study that analyzed 172 married couples over the first eleven years of marriage, UCLA psychologists reported that a deep level of commitment is a good predictor of lower divorce rates and fewer problems in marriage.[6]
- Research suggests the more couples experience "self-expansion" in marriage (where both partners encourage the self-development of their spouse), the more committed and satisfied they are in the relationship.
- Good marriage relationships are built on learning to listen and talk well.

- Looking for new topics that interest both you and your partner leads to interesting discussion.
- Laughing together is strong relational glue.
- Common faith commitments contribute to a unified approach to life.

To enjoy a lifelong happy marriage, couples need to be clear about what commitments they bring to the marriage that will enable them to go the distance. For example, are they willing to commit to making the satisfaction of the other person as important to them as their own?

A big block to long-term commitment is temperament. It is not long before we realize that the other person is very different from what we are—different ways of thinking and doing things. A common assumption is that in happy marriages the couple is like-minded. Yet in my own marriage, although Janiece and I share common values and are very happy, we are quite opposite in many ways. Which way is "right"—linear or creative thinking, traditional or innovative orientation, thoughtful or impulsive behavior, introvert or extrovert positioning? Constantly trying to change the other doesn't work. We found it best to see the beauty in each temperament.

At dinner in one of our favorite restaurants, Janiece and I heard some lyrics over the sound system that I think went like this:

I am me. I am me. I am me.
You are you. You are you. You are you.
Oh, well.

An "Oh, well" resignation to nonessential differences may be the best response. Janiece and I aim for humor when our temperaments collide—although I must be careful to laugh *with*, not *at* her. What keeps us enjoying each other goes way beyond our temperaments. We are committed to making the satisfaction of the other as important as our own. We aim for an essential marital unity based on common values, aims, and beliefs. So we give each other space, the freedom to be who we are. We are like two sides of one coin.

Marriage Values to Share

Marital unity is hard work, but it's the hard work that makes the relationship work and adds value to life. Unity results from an effort of the heart, mind, and will of a couple. Each affirms the other as the most important person on earth to them. Marital unity does not cling; it provides space in the midst of togetherness. It's a bond that provides freedom, a commitment that engenders trust. It puts you on the happiness path.

Strong marriages possess many of the following values. These values provide a checklist for the readiness of a protégé for marriage.

_____ Commitment based on mutual trust, honesty, and respect
_____ Physical attraction
_____ Similar work interests
_____ Integrity; doing what you say
_____ Intellectual compatibility
_____ Belief in marriage as a lifelong commitment
_____ The desire to talk and listen well
_____ Similar goals for family, work, finances, and lifestyle
_____ An eagerness to resolve conflicts and forgive
_____ The ability to laugh together
_____ A developing love communicated daily in ways that please the partner
_____ A shared faith the couple practices together.

Marriage Questions to Ask

You may want to begin discussion with your protégé by telling what you learned from your own experience. Include the humor, mistakes, feelings, and hopes, but don't get too carried away talking about *your* past. It's easy to do, and your talk could seem to last "forever" to the protégé. Encourage the youth you mentor to ask *their* questions. You might not agree with their thoughts and actions, but at least you have an opportunity to discuss them. Instead of contradicting the teen, you could say, "The way I see it is...." You then have the possibility of making a difference.

As you prepare your own list of questions to discuss, consider the following:

- What qualities do you want in your marriage partner?
- What does "love" or "respecting the other" mean to you?
- To what extent is your relationship characterized by seeking the satisfaction and well-being of your partner?
- What will you do when there is a difference of opinion, such as where to live or work, children, responsibilities, parents, etc.
- How well do your financial and vocational aspirations fit with those of your friend?
- Why do you think your marriage will be successful?
- How does your faith affect how you approach this relationship?

As you mentor youth in these four major decision areas— Education, Vocation, Money, and Marriage—one area may stand out as being the most important. Add other topics if they are pertinent. Talk about them all, even briefly, because the few thoughts you convey could prevent the serious hurt and frustration of your protégé walking down the wrong path. The positive difference you can make through mentoring a person younger than you is beyond measure.

By mentoring, you serve. You not only help youth move in a purposeful direction, you experience the special happiness that comes from influencing goodness in the lives of the next generation. Your sense of life satisfaction is deepened.

CLARIFY YOUR LIFE PURPOSE

Chapter 8

*What makes life worthwhile is having a big
enough objective, something which catches our
imagination and lays hold of our allegiance...*

—J. I. Packer

How many people do you know who have a vital purpose for their lives—an objective that grabs their imagination and calls forth their special talents? A more important question is: do you?

In my junior year of college, I did not have a clear purpose. I panicked from one major to another. I knew I wanted to do something worthwhile, but nothing seemed to fit. Eventually I wandered into a path that was right for me, but I wasted a lot of time and had some anxious moments.

This chapter helps you draw a blueprint that will fit your life's dimensions. Your building materials are your past and present experiences, your hopes for the future, your relationships and your abilities. When you have gathered this information, you will be able to construct your own one-sentence purpose statement. You will relate to others better because you will feel more confident about why you are here and where you are going.

Defining Moments

To begin the process, think about moments that have defined who you are—memories that sadden or delight you. Defining moments may also include encouraging statements by family, teachers, or friends. You will be energized as you consider what has shaped you, what guides you now, and what you want your future to be like.

Introspection or self-examination might be a new skill for you, but try it. Grab your laptop or piece of paper and jot down your memories and hopes.

Your Past: What have been the five most defining moments in your life?

Your Present: What up to now has been your goal in life, if any?

Your Future: What do you want your future to be like?

Your answers make clear what has influenced you so far. But as you continue your process toward building a purpose or life mission statement, those answers will clarify who you want to be and the changes you need to make to reach your destination.

Governing Values

When you face a fork in the road, how do you know what direction to take? Values guide you. Values are like the North Star; they serve as a reliable point of reference. Fashions change, but the fixed reference that values give you provides far-reaching benefits:

- Clarity—values help you know what matters most.
- Focus—values help you know where you need to realign priorities.
- Discernment—values help you make the right choices.

So, what values are important to you? Honesty? Peace? Hope? Loyalty? To gain clarity about what you are passionate about, write down three to five values you want to govern your life. As you clarify these values, you reinforce their importance to you. You take a giant step toward discovering your purpose.

Key Roles and Relationships

Roles represent relationships—who you are in relation to others. In each relationship your responsibilities may differ. For example, you function differently as a friend than as an employee, team leader, parent, student, or spouse. It will help to jot down all your current roles.

Abilities and Strengths

Have you ever thought about what special talents you have, what you are really good at? What do other people say you do well? What do you most enjoy doing?

You are an extraordinary bundle of possibilities even though you might not be aware of them all. But the fact that you don't know everything about yourself doesn't mean you know nothing. You likely understand yourself better than most. You might be gifted in a particular area or two—for example: Encourager; Peacemaker;

Intellectual; Listener; Creative. Write down some of the strengths you think you have or people say you have.

Criteria for Your Purpose

So far you have thought about your defining moments, governing values, key roles, and abilities. This thinking is foundational. Now on this foundation you can build a purpose statement that will inspire you.

As you prepare to write down your ideas in the next section, first check all the following guidelines you want to characterize your purpose statement.

- Is consistent with who you are and who you want to be.
- Defines the significant difference you want to make.
- Frees you from unimportant details to do what you find liberating.
- Rewards you internally regardless of any financial payment you receive.
- Motivates you even when no one notices or seems to be impressed.
- Enables you to experience life fully.

Purpose Statement

Your purpose statement is unique to you. Initially it may sound similar to other purpose statements, but eventually it will reflect your special self. And if it's to motivate you throughout your life, it might sound really big now.

Victor Frankl, a psychiatrist who survived Nazi prison camps, found that although prisoners experienced the same conditions, some died whereas others lived. Those who lived had exercised their choice to live because they believed they had a purpose to fulfill. Those who died generally let physical conditions and mental despair snuff out their lives. Frankl concluded that the person who had a *why* (a meaningful task to fulfill) could withstand almost any *how* (negative condition). He wrote:

> *There is nothing in the world, I dare say, which would so effectively help man to survive and keep healthy as would the knowledge of a life task.*[1]

Early on, my father wanted me to see the big picture of life. With the wisdom of experience, he transferred to me the concept of a purpose-driven life—a purpose that encompassed all of life. He would say, "Son, our chief purpose is to glorify God and enjoy Him forever."[2] Although I did not fully understand the lesson, I was awed by how big it was. It took root in my thinking because I saw my dad live out that viewpoint in his life even in the worst of times.

Let's see how this all comes together for you. Grab your laptop, a piece of paper, or write in the margins of this book. It might take several drafts until you feel really good about what you've written, so don't hesitate to scribble whatever comes to mind. You can change it later as you wish. Complete each of the following parts of your purpose statement based on the thinking you've done.

My most important purpose in life is to....
in my roles of....
guided by my values of....
through my abilities and strengths to....
that will result in....

Check all the items below that apply to your purpose statement. My purpose:

_____ anchors me to what I believe

_____ is what I really want in life

_____ is consistent with my greatest strengths

_____ relates to significance more than to cultural success

_____ could easily be described as my personal life passion

_____ may be realized more in the future than it is now

_____ stabilizes my decision making

Let the celebration begin! Now you have your beginning statement of what's important to you. If someone does not share your excitement, that's okay. Your purpose needs to reflect your big picture and who *you* are—that growing, developing, rejuvenated you. In the weeks ahead, you may rewrite your purpose so it better represents your core. In the meantime, you are on your way to experiencing a new kind of direction, fulfillment, and happiness.

PART FOUR:
CELEBRATING HOPE

Rejoice in hope!

—St. Paul

L ife can be overwhelming. We can be worn down by anxiety
about what *might* happen, frustration about goals not met, and
the constant demands of life. Hope reverses that trend by enabling
us to look forward to a brighter future, in spite of our circumstances.

In Part Four, we look at what psychologists call the "psyche" and
theologians call the "soul." Who we are on the inside can be changed
by the way we *think* about ourselves and the future. St. Paul says, "Be
transformed by the renewing of your mind."[1]

Renewing our minds enables us to see the really big picture—
where history is headed and the destination of our own lives. That's
why Paul is able to say, "Rejoice in hope!" Although hope is an emotion
deep within, it anchors the soul and shows in our relationships. We
are more relaxed, more confident, more able to see beyond the flaws
in our friends and ourselves. Hope provides a foundation for joy now.

Experiencing hope is a happiness worth celebrating!

CHOOSE A NEW YOU

Chapter 9

The more we let God take us over,
the more truly ourselves we become—
because He made us. He invented us....
When I give up myself to His personality,
I first begin to have a real personality of my own.

—C. S. Lewis

"Who are you?"

People want to know who we really are, but the question "Who are you?" is a bit too personal. So they ask, "What do you do?" The question usually refers to our work activity and serves as a polite way of getting to know us better because our work influences how others categorize us. But consider this—our work can also influence how *we categorize ourselves.*

Does the work category adequately represent who we are? From the death camps of World War II, psychiatrist Victor Frankl discovered that we can transcend the level of our "psychic and physical conditions." Even when we feel trapped by our past work or imprisoned in a present job, transformational change is available.

Transformation can be seen as an "outside" and "inside" operation. Whereas the outside operation concerns what you *do*, the inside operation primarily concerns who you *are*. Both have deep and wide implications. Both require wise responses to stimuli.

Doing What You Choose to Do

Who controls what you do? An important moment for me was the realization that at a certain level, I can choose what I do. I can choose to go to work or not go. I can choose a particular subject to study or some other. Kind of basic. Right? Even as a youth, I was already making decisions that affected the direction of my life. I chose what I did.

A crucial moment for me came when I developed a mental foundation for my ability to choose. I remember learning the S-R theory, which states that if you control the *stimulus*, you control the *result*. Psychologist Pavlov is known for his experimentation with dogs to prove the S-R theory. When the dogs heard a bell ring (stimulus), they began to salivate (response). The stimulus-response predictability became a key part of a theory of human behavior called "Behaviorism."[1]

We do respond in predictable ways to much of the stimuli we face—when we see a police car behind us, we slow down; when we place our hand on a hot stove, we instantly respond without thinking about it. You likely can add examples from your own behavioral tendencies.

We can diagram this type of behavior as follows:

Stimulus → Response

Granted, a stimulus often produces a highly accurate response. But what about the bigger issues of our lives, like choosing our future or becoming the person we really want to be? Are we limited only to an S-R type of existence as some suppose?

I don't think so. Actually, the S-R theory suggests severe limits to our freedom. But surely humans can respond with intelligent choices beyond stimulus-controlled reactions. Although S-R does explain some behavior, it says nothing about our ability to choose a different response. A more accurate description for humans can be described as follows:

Stimulus → **Choice** → Response

Norman Cousins writes in *Human Options* that choosing is a special gift of mankind: "The human species is unique because it alone can create, recognize, and exercise options…. It is part of human experience that we are endowed with the faculty of choice."[2]

Stephen Covey, author of *7 Habits of Highly Successful People*, writes that this concept of human choice also had a profound impact on his life and was a fundamental concept in his writing of the *7 Habits*. One day in a library, he read three sentences that "staggered him to the core."

> *Between stimulus and response there is a space. In that space lies our freedom and power to choose our response. In those choices lie our growth and our happiness.*[3]

When you review your past, perhaps you notice that certain stimuli (people, situations, job environment) have influenced you to respond in a way that is unwise and contrary to the person you want to be. You might say that a negative stimulus produced an unwise response. But what has been in the past does not determine your future. You can change a negative behavior pattern by choosing what you truly want to do. It looks like this:

Negative Stimulus → **Choice** → Positive Response

When negative influences are intercepted by wise choices, we are in a better position to make forward progress toward what matters to us. This is huge! The ability to choose positively impacts how we live.

If you have made unwise choices in the past, you can start today to choose wisely. In the short run, a wise choice (such as doing the honest thing at work) might have negative effects (you might lose your job). But I have never ever seen a person who consistently makes wise choices regret the consequences long-term. Have you? Wise choices have their own intrinsic reward.

Choosing to Become a New You

What is the wisest choice you can make regarding who you want to become? You are not tied to other people's expectations. You are not limited by what you do or have been. You can choose to become a new you.

Did you know that becoming a new you can set you on a path to new freedom? It's a freedom linked to your core being, your psyche, your soul. And when your soul is free, you are free indeed. Even financially poor people who know "soul freedom" show happiness. They enjoy an inner freedom not controlled by external events.

Inner freedom to become all you were created to be requires a transformation of your soul. The Bible states that transformational change is accomplished by a faith relationship with Christ, who rescues us from anything that binds us. Apostle Paul wrote, "For freedom Christ has set us free."[4]

If you sense a need to be free from all that enslaves—a need for a fullness in life that money, status, and interpersonal relationships cannot fill—choose God. Choose to answer God's call to you to believe, choose to center your life in your relationship with God.

God's call to us is something of a mystery. Why would the Creator of the universe care about mankind—about you and me? Psalmist King David asked that question:

> *I look up at your macro-skies, dark and enormous,*
> *Your handmade sky-jewelry,*
> *Moon and stars mounted in their settings.*
> *Then I look at my micro-self and wonder,*
> *Why do you bother with us?*
> *Why take a second look our way?*[5]

I wonder about that. You, too?

Ponder this—a secure relationship with an all-powerful God who loves you. Is this not what everyone wants? Blaise Pascal, mathematician, philosopher, and Christ follower, said, "There is a God-shaped vacuum in the heart of every person which cannot be filled by any created thing, but only by God, the Creator, made known through Jesus."[6]

Wait a minute! Can that be proven? No, it's a gamble. Pascal explains:

> *Belief is a wise wager. Granted that faith cannot be proved, what harm will come to you if you gamble on its truth and it proves false?*

If you gain, you gain all; if you lose, you lose nothing. Wager, then, without hesitation, that He exists.[7]

By "wager," Pascal is not suggesting we depend on faith *instead* of reason, but that after a person uses faith and reason in the search for God, there is a point where reason can go no farther. Faith, based on God's revelation in the Bible, leaps forward.

Dean Overman, author of *A Case for the Existence of God,* affirmed that "Although theism requires a leap of faith, it is a leap into the light, not into the dark; theism explains more than atheism, which also requires a leap of faith."[8]

A defining moment in the life of British journalist Malcolm Muggeridge came when he acknowledged to himself that he did not want God. He was afraid that God would change his lifestyle and replace it with something inferior. He writes:

Is there a God? Well, is there? I myself should be very happy to answer with an emphatic negative. Temperamentally, it would suit me well enough to settle for what this world offers, and to write off as wishful thinking, or just the self-importance of the human species, any notion of a divine purpose and a divinity to entertain and execute it.[9]

But after reviewing common paths to happiness (material things, power, status, sex, popularity), Muggeridge concluded that any satisfaction brought by them is short-lived. He could not ignore what he sensed—that although he did not want God in his life, *God wanted him.*[10]

Muggeridge's initial resistance to a relationship with God illustrates our natural tendency to put self, or anything else, in the vacuum only God can fill. The Bible calls that tendency sin; we disobey the first commandment to "have no other gods before me."[11]

If our highest allegiance is to self or family or nation or race, we not only minimize who we are, we actually contribute to the destruction of the social fabric. We become egocentric or nationalistic or racist. Only if God is our highest good will we find our hearts drawn to people of all families, races, and nations.[12]

Discovering a New Identity

If God wants to be in a personal relationship with you, do you want to resist? Think for a moment about times when you were selected for something. Is there not happiness in being "wanted," in being chosen because you are valued as a person? Imagine yourself *chosen by the Creator of the universe*, not because of what you can do or have done, but simply because God values you.

I find immense joy in being chosen or valued by God. It's a happiness rooted in being free from anything that separates and diminishes. It's delight in a relationship with God. It's satisfaction in pursuing a worthwhile life task. All this personal freedom is available to anyone through faith in Christ. Apostle Paul claims that anyone who follows Christ has a new identity. When Christ is at the center, you become a "new person."[13]

NFL quarterback Peyton Manning, voted "Sportsman of the Year" by *Sports Illustrated* in 2013, described how he came to faith.

> *My faith has been number one since I was thirteen years old and heard from the pulpit on a Sunday morning in New Orleans a simple question: "If you died today, are you one hundred percent sure you'd go to heaven?"… It was a big church and I felt very small, but my heart was pounding. The minister invited those who would like that*

assurance to raise their hands, and I did…. And I committed my life to Christ, and that faith has been most important to me ever since.[14]

Distinguishing Choices

So what is a new person in Christ like? Unfortunately not all followers of Christ connect their faith to their actions. But in those who do, I've noticed a few distinguishing features that characterize the "new person" in Christ.

Purpose: Christ followers aim first of all to glorify God and enjoy him forever. This single purpose moves them to explore the deepest, highest, grandest reason for being born. Whether this purpose includes playing football, serving the country, teaching youth, or washing dishes, it dynamically integrates who they are called to be with what they are created to do.

Sociologist Max Weber noticed that the seventeenth and eighteenth century Puritans worked diligently for the glory of God. Their purpose in doing the right thing, even when no one was looking, was part of their devotion to God. The result? Business owners noticed their dependability and promoted them. Puritans often became wealthy even though wealth was not their life goal; wealth was an indirect result of their purpose to please God.[15]

Calmness: St. Augustine, philosopher, theologian, and writer in the fourth century, searched desperately for inner peace. In his own experience, he discovered a deep chaos that only God could transform. He confessed to God, "Our souls are restless until they find their rest in You."[16]

Through the years I've talked with hundreds of believers who possessed a tranquility beyond understanding even on their deathbed or in tragic situations; a calm center evident even in the midst of trying circumstances.

To be calm with danger all around is difficult. It takes conscious discipline to link our beliefs, feelings, and behavior. When we don't link them well, we lose mental muscle to be calm; we develop attitudes not anchored to anything firm; controlled by whatever way the social wind blows.

Internal calm is not automatic. Peace is given to believers who ask for it and *act* on it. An attitude of peacefulness results from a dynamic relationship with God[17] that engenders a sense of safety, well-being, wholeness, completeness, tranquility, unity, harmony, happiness— like a young child happily whistling in the dark, but holding tight the father's hand.

Boldness: How we react to danger is undoubtedly related to our temperament (e.g., anxious vs fearless tendencies). But if we choose to act on the mystery of God's sovereignty in our lives, if we experience an enduring calmness holding the Father's hand, we can face anything.

Think about this: if God is really *for* us,[18] what actual difference does it make if some person doesn't like this or that about us? If our eternal destiny is secure, are the gyrations of the stock market or poor health or even death something to worry much about? Obviously we should do everything in our power to meet the challenges of life.

But to constantly *worry*? Not if we choose attitudes that connect our *beliefs* about the future with our *feelings* and *actions*.

Gratitude: Cicero said "Gratitude is not only the greatest of virtues, but the parent of all others."[19] When we begin our day with gratitude to God, it instructs other attitudes for the rest of the day. For instance, the attitude of thanksgiving leads us to look for God's blessing all around us. *Blessings* are seen as everyday sacred cryptograms that generate happiness. Christians actually view these blessings as gifts provided by a gracious heavenly Father.

Gospel writer Luke reports the gratitude of a man Jesus healed.

> *Taking a good look at them, he said, "Go, show yourselves to the priests." They went, and while still on their way, became clean. One of them, when he realized that he was healed, turned around and came back, shouting his gratitude, glorifying God. He kneeled at Jesus' feet, so grateful. He couldn't thank him enough—and he was a Samaritan.*[20]

Love: When a person experiences the love of God, it generates warm regard for others not tied to getting something back from them. That "regard" is like a poor person helping a wealthy person in need without expecting anything in return.

Love like this drives individuals to seek the well-being of those around them; to get out of their comfort zone to right wrongs and to help those in need. These individuals seem compelled to decrease social evils, such as human trafficking, and to care for the dispossessed, sick, and dying. When you meet them, you likely will want them as friends because they look for the goodness in you.

Joy: In my own travels in Siberia, Kenya, Tanzania, Uganda, Netherlands, England, and the United States, I observed a common depth of joy in believers in a variety of circumstances. Joy was expressed not only by those who possessed material abundance, but also by those in poverty and living very near death. I remember hearing Canon Andrew White, known as the "Bishop of Baghdad," talk about his encounters with daily tragedy while leading his congregation in Iraq. He said the dominant emotion of his people is *joy*.[21] Canon White remarked, "They have nothing, but they have everything, because they have Jesus... because Jesus is the center of their lives."[22]

In the Hebrew Scripture, the Psalmist calls everyone to make a joyful sound to the Lord.[23] Apostle Paul repeatedly reminds believers to rejoice[24] because of the gospel.[25] Jesus told a story about a woman who, when she found her lost treasure, threw a party for her friends. Jesus said "Just so, I tell you, there is joy before the angels of God over one sinner who repents."[26] (Repentance is confessing that our lives have gone in the wrong direction and that we want to be transformed into a follower of Christ.)

To further illustrate the joy that follows repentance, Jesus told a story about a son who was "lost," squandering his wealth in reckless living, and then "found," after coming to his senses. The biblical record says that when the son finally realized his sin against God and his father, he turned for home. The father welcomed him with open arms... and they all began to "make merry."[27] Jesus' point: *the Heavenly Father is like that*!

You might wonder: *Would God welcome me?* Yes, certainly! For a dramatic account of my daughter and her husband's pain being "lost" and their joy of being "found," go to YouTube and insert: www.movingworks.org/project/raised.[28]

Perhaps you have noticed these qualities in people with no faith as well as faith. Admittedly these merits are not exclusive to believers and, yes, there are plenty of religious people who abuse the rights of others. Yet there seems to be a distinctive common core that radiates these qualities (and more) in persons who show active faith in Jesus.

Genuine "faith in Jesus" does not mean the same as "belonging to a certain church." In fact, the linkage is not primarily institutional—a "church member" might not be a Christ follower. Rather, "faith in Jesus" refers to a vigorous relationship with God that is actually *astounding* to the believer. It often overflows in humble exuberance, an inner joy, an enduring happiness.

We have considered how sometimes we define ourselves by our work or our past. We limit ourselves when we think "in-the-box" of what has been. But we break out of that box by choosing to become a new person through faith in God, made known through Jesus Christ. Through the work of Christ in us, we are transformed. We are *reborn* inside. We experience a revitalized center that empowers us to see other people and the whole world in a fresh way.

Do you want to become a new person on the inside? The process is simple yet profound. The simple part is saying "Yes!" to God's call for you to "come home," to be transformed through faith in God so you look at people and life now *sub specie aeternitatis*—under the viewpoint of eternity. It's the most profound choice you can make because as the Bible says, you become a "friend of God," the One who gives you eternal hope.

A medical doctor friend and I visited Sergei in a hospice hospital when we were on a mission trip in Siberia. Sergei wore a cross on a chain. I said, "Tell me about why you wear a cross."

With the help of a translator, he replied, "My mother gave me this cross more than seventy years ago. She said Russia would face very difficult years ahead, but in the end there would be hope."

I said, "Sergei, do you have hope that when you die you will go to heaven?"

He said, "No, I will go to hell!" I asked him if he would like to know he could go to heaven.

He answered "Yes!"

My doctor friend and I shared the gospel with him and he prayed to receive Christ into his life.[29] Then he said, "My mother was right. It is the end for me, but now I have hope."

When you become a new person through faith in Christ, you begin experiencing a new confidence for life now. You find vibrant happiness for eternity. Wow!

LIVE WITH THE END
IN MIND

Chapter 10

The end is where we start from.

—T.S. Eliot

P ersons believing in Christ walk toward a new destination, an
endpoint that assures eternal happiness. The end of this life is
viewed as the beginning of life after death—a big picture that informs
our perspectives and choices. It's the end "where we start from."

In *The Pursuit of Happiness*, Psychologist David Myers reflects, "If
I can believe that my long-term destiny is in God's loving hands, then
I can cope with whatever awaits me from now till death. I can trust
that, come what may, all will turn out well in the end, the very end."[1]

Followers of Christ look at the very end of this life *sub specie
aeternitatis,* "under the viewpoint of the eternal." And it makes all
the difference in the world today.

Joy is one difference. For literary critic and former agnostic C.
S. Lewis, this difference was a huge surprise. Lewis felt compelled
by his search for truth to convert from disbelief to faith in God. But
after his conversion, he was stunned to discover that an exhilarating

happiness encompassed him. Lewis remarked that he was "surprised by joy."[2]

Joy in the Context of Death

Can joy be sustained even in the face of death? Sometimes we get rumors of what's ahead for us personally through the results of a health condition, an accident report, or the death of a loved one.

A near-death experience shook my own perspective. One day I thought myself to be healthy; the next day I found myself in the emergency room with a sharp pain in my chest. When I asked the nurse how my blood pressure numbers were looking, she said, "You're having a heart attack!" After a five-bypass surgery I was still alive, but no longer able to do what I once did.

Have you ever been close to death? Samuel Johnson, one of the most quoted men of the eighteenth century, once remarked that when a person knows he is about to die, it wonderfully concentrates his mind. With intense concentration, I asked myself questions I had asked when I first started my journey of faith:

- What's ahead?
- Is there a God?
- Is heaven real?

As I honestly reflected on these questions, I found God's *rescue plan* for life to be trustworthy, even joy-producing.

C.S. Lewis, reviewing his own journey from agnosticism to faith, concluded, "Joy is the serious business of heaven."[3] He suggested that most of us don't take this joy seriously. He had not.

It would seem that Our Lord finds our desires not too strong, but too weak. We are half-hearted creatures, fooling about with drink and sex and ambition when infinite joy is offered us, like an ignorant child who wants to go on making mud pies in a slum because he cannot imagine what is meant by the offer of a holiday at the sea. We are far too easily pleased.[4]

Snatching Victory from Defeat

Our enemies (sin and death) are brutal. There seems to be no end to their pervasive cruelty. Suffering dominates. Perhaps you wonder how you could live *sub specie aeternitatis,* "under the viewpoint of eternity," in a world where life is not fair and many people you know are hurting.

My friend Moses, an immigrant from Sudan, had worked hard to provide for his wife and five children. One day he called me to say his apartment had burned and everything in it was destroyed. Then, while recovering from the fire, he also learned he had serious health issues, possibly jeopardizing his ability to provide for his family. Sustained by his relationship with God, he said, "God knows my heart and the condition of my family. I am a new person in Christ. My wife and children are concerned, but whatever happens is not a surprise to God. We lost man-made things, but not what God has given us—faith, hope, and love. I am at peace."

Peace this strong turns defeat into victory. Faith, hope, and love win.

Reinhold Niebuhr, pastor and theologian, states in *Beyond Tragedy* that the good news of Christian faith is a message of hope in the midst of tragedy. "The God of Christian faith is not only creator but redeemer. He does not allow human existence to end tragically. He snatches victory from defeat."[5]

Victory over all that would defeat us is accomplished by Jesus' death on a cross and resurrection to life. Jesus, as both God in flesh and representative man, was able to take upon himself that penalty our selfish choices deserve. Jesus gives forgiveness to all who believe in him.[6] Niebuhr comments,

> Without the cross men are beguiled by what is good in human existence into a false optimism and by what is tragic into despair. The message of the Son of God who dies upon the cross, of a God who transcends history and is yet in history, who condemns and judges sin and yet suffers with and for the sinner, this message is the truth about life.[7]

God's rescue action through the death of Christ on the cross offers to us extravagant goodness—a goodness that does not rest upon *us* earning God's favor (resulting in the notion that our good deeds must outweigh the bad), but upon *God*. It is only by God's grace, demonstrated in the cross, that we are saved through faith in Christ. Though much in the world now is not good, Niebuhr states that Christian faith is trust in "a good God, powerful and good enough finally to destroy the evil that men do and redeem them of their sins."[8]

Persons who contemplate and act upon such redemption reflect the light of Christ even in dark times.

Rescued Attitudes

What difference would it make in your life if you were pulled free from certain destruction in a burning house? If you've ever been burned by the fire of injustice or cruelty or betrayal by someone you trusted—and then were refreshed from inside by a relationship with God—you would likely experience grateful jubilation. I do.

Unfortunately, not all believers demonstrate rescued attitudes. When Christ followers don't realize the extent of their rescue, they allow themselves to be controlled by the concerns of this world. Yet when they do act on the *abundant life*[9] Christ came to give his followers, the logical response is joy.

Easter offers a big enough foundation for cosmic joy. If Easter means Jesus Christ is truly risen from the dead, as Scripture proclaims, then as professor N. T. Wright remarks,

> *Christianity becomes good news for the whole world—news which warms our hearts precisely because it isn't just about warming hearts. Easter means that in a world where injustice is endemic, God is not prepared to tolerate such things—and that we will work and plan, with all the energy of God, to implement victory of Jesus over them all.*[10]

Well-being flourishes when we develop the relational skills needed for strong friendships, connect well with those closest to us, live with a purpose that energizes us to gratefully give back what we alone can give, and face our future with reasoned optimism anchored by hope.

Dear reader, as we come to the end of our thinking together, may I offer you a "blessing"—a happiness causing truth? This blessing comes from Apostle Paul:

> *May the God of hope fill you with all joy and peace in believing, so that by the power of the Holy Spirit you may abound in hope.* [11]

Abounding in hope that is real and true provides an anchor to steady our restless souls; a hope that leads us to God. [12]

Laughter is enriched.

Happiness is found.

Hallelujah! [13]

ACKNOWLEDGMENTS

*F*inding Happiness would never have been published if it were not for a number of individuals who have influenced my life through the years and patiently guided me in this labor of love. I am deeply grateful for each one.

Bill and Ethel Swets—my parents who demonstrated daily to my five sisters and me the meaning of abundant life.

Janiece Swets—my wife and best friend who developed astute editing skills and somehow managed the very difficult task of being a tough critic and my strongest cheerleader.

Judson Swets and Jessica Swets Roberts, our children who as teenagers challenged my wife and me to use our best communication skills and who now heartily and lovingly undertake the task of leading their children into a remarkable future.

Ethelanne, Marcia, Karen, Faith, and Mary—my sisters who taught me the value of close communication in the family.

Rich DeVos—an extraordinary entrepreneur who encouraged me greatly with his positive and giving spirit, and who along with Jay

Van Andel and the Amway Corporation taught me the disciplines necessary to succeed.

Professors Robert De Haan and Robert Brown at Hope College, Lester Kuyper and Jim Cook at Western Theological Seminary, and Marvin Felheim and Richard Young at the University of Michigan—mentors who taught me to search for truth and develop a global world-and-life view.

Alex Mouw, Josh Kamstra, Forrest Dodson, Amy Van Dommelen, and Katie Cutshall—students at Hope College who poured many hours of their expertise into helping me improve the manuscript.

Sandy Willson, Jon Brown, and Chris DeVos—pastors who have touched my heart, guided my soul, and repeatedly enriched my relationship with God.

Mark Hiskes—a friend, educator, and influencer of thousands of young minds.

Max DePree, Gordon Van Wylen, Harold Gazan, Jim Neevel, George Hoekstra, Frank and Sue Pettinga, Harry Visscher, and Jim and Susan Boersma—among the many friends in my living community whose questions and personal support helped me through the writing process.

Finally, I want to thank the One who literally transformed my life, my Savior and Lord, Jesus Christ, who said, "I have come in order that you might have life and have it abundantly" (John 10:10), and "These things I have spoken to you, that my joy may be in you, and that your joy may be full" (John 15:11).

It is Jesus' gift of "abundant life" and "joy" that has resulted in joy in the core of my being and motivates me to share how anyone can find lasting happiness.

ABOUT THE AUTHOR

G rowing up in a large family with five sisters, Paul Swets learned how important effective communication was in producing harmony. Through counseling others and through his research, he learned that real understanding was possible and that when achieved, life could be experienced more joyfully.

Dr. Swets' lifelong passion to make a difference in peoples' lives began with some serious study. His major in college, psychology, helped him understand individual behavior more fully. He mastered in American culture to study how our environment shapes personal thought. He studied theology to understand better a person's relationship to God. He earned a doctorate in effective communication at the University of Michigan to determine how individuals can better relate to one another.

Wanting to share the good news with as many people as possible, Paul felt called to enter the ministry. With his wife and family, he served churches in Ann Arbor Michigan, West Palm Beach Florida, and Memphis Tennessee.

Paul's wife, Janiece, is an expert in caring communication. She works with Paul to bring out the best in people. They are grateful to still be best friends through forty-plus years of marriage.

Now Paul and Janiece celebrate everyday life in Holland Michigan with a great community of friends.

For further information, go to http://findinghappiness.info.

NOTES

PREFACE: YOU CAN EXPERIENCE LASTING HAPPINESS!

1. Jeffrey Kluger, "The Pursuit of Happiness," *Time* Magazine, May 20, 2013, 24.
2. David G. Myers, *The Pursuit of Happiness: Who is Happy and Why* (New York: William Morrow, 1992), 31–46.
3. Ibid. After massive research, Myers wrote the poem about unsuccessful efforts in the pursuit of happiness.
4. Robert Holden, "The Gift of Happiness" in *Resurgence* magazine, November/December, 2011.
5. Happiness research is a relatively new focus in psychological study. Instead of a concentration on depression and abnormal behavior, positive psychology maintains that an aspect of happiness called Subjective Well-Being (SWB) can be empirically measured. This focus has opened the door to exciting new research about what contributes to SWB around the world. Here are a few examples of recent investigations:

   • Ed Diener, *Happiness: Unlocking the Mysteries of Psychological Wealth*, Malden MA: Oxford: Blackwell Publishers, 2008. While income is not highly correlated with happiness, Diener found that social relationships are.

- Shawn Achor, *The Happiness Advantage*, NY: Crown Business, 2010. Achor's book is a report that change is possible. That's the "happiness advantage."
- Ellen Charry, *God and the Art of Happiness*, Grand Rapids MI: Eerdmans, 2010. Charry shows how the Bible encourages authentic happiness and flourishing that accompany obedience to the Creator.
- Frieda Klotz, "Happiness is the New Success: Why Millennials Are Reprioritizing," *Forbes Woman* 2/24/2012.

6. Ed Diener in a documentary video on happiness research entitled "Happy."

CHAPTER 2: LISTEN SO PEOPLE TALK

1. The three barriers to listening on pages 18 and 19 are adapted and updated from Paul Swets, *The Art of Talking So That People Will Listen* (New York: Simon & Schuster, 1992), 41–42.
2. Joel Stein, "The ME ME ME Generation," *Time* Magazine, July 8, 2013, 26.
3. Saundra Hybels and Richard Weaver II, *Communicating Effectively*, University of Illinois: Textbook, 2014.
4. University of Virginia Health System, *"Pitch-Detection Secrets of the Inner Ear Revealed by Science,"* May 2014.
5. Paul Swets, *The Art of Talking So That People Will Listen* (New York: Simon & Schuster, 1992), 48.
6. Joseph T. Bayly, *The Last Thing We Talk About* (Illinois: D. C. Cook, 1969), 40–41, quoted in Swets, 50.

CHAPTER 3: TALK SO PEOPLE LISTEN

1. Yogi Berra. Favorite quotations of Yogi Berra.
2. Paul Swets, *The Art of Talking So That People Will Listen* (New York: Simon & Schuster, 1992), 20.
3. Here are Professor Albert Mehrabian's results from his communication research: Words (Verbal) 7%; Tone (Vocal) 38%; Posture (Visual) 55%. How did you do?
4. Swets, xi.
5. C. S. Lewis, *The Great Divorce,* New York: Macmillan, 1970.

CHAPTER 4: RESOLVE CONFLICTS

1. The Conflict Resolution Model was developed in Paul Swets, *The Art of Talking So That People Will Listen* (New York: Simon & Schuster, 1992), 142. It is amplified and updated here for the purpose of this book.

CHAPTER 5: CREATE CLOSENESS

1. Dr. Martin Luther King, Jr. quote on Forgiveness.
2. English *Standard Version* (Wheaton, IL: Cross Way Bibles, 2008), Matthew 6:12, 14–15.
3. *Stephen* M.R. Covey, *The Speed of Trust* (New York: Free Press, 2006), 1–2.
4. *English Standard Version,* Wheaton, IL: Cross Way Bibles, 2008), Genesis 2:25.
5. *English Standard Version,* Wheaton, IL: Cross Way Bibles, 2008), Proverbs 16:32.

6. A participant in a *Closeness Through Communication* seminar conducted by Paul and Janiece Swets. Used by permission.
7. *English Standard Version,* Wheaton, IL: Cross Way Bibles, 2008), Proverbs 11:12.
8. *English Standard Version,* Wheaton, IL: Cross Way Bibles, 2008), 1 Thessalonians 5:11.
9. *English Standard Version,* Wheaton, IL: Cross Way Bibles, 2008), Proverbs 15:4.
10. Richard M. DeVos, *Ten Powerful Phrases for Positive People,* New York: Center Street, 2008.

CHAPTER 6: SUSTAIN FRIENDSHIPS

1. Thomas Bradbury reporting on a new study from the UCLA Relationship Center, 2012.
2. "Commitments that Sustain Friendship" has been adapted and updated from Paul Swets, *The Art of Talking So That People Will Listen* (New York: Simon & Schuster, 1992), 131.
3. Harry Stack Sullivan, *Personal Psychopathology,* New York: W. W. Norton, 1984.
4. Gretchen Rubin, in a blog related to her book, *The Happiness Project,* New York: HarperCollins, 2012.

CHAPTER 7: MENTOR OTHER WITH LESS EXPERIENCE

1. English *Standard Version* (Wheaton, IL: Cross Way Bibles, 2008), Proverbs 2:1–5.
2. John R. Schneider, *The Good of Affluence* (Grand Rapids, Michigan: William B. Eerdmans Publishing Company, 2002), 3.

3. Lee Atwater's reflections on wealth.
4. Harry Stack Sullivan, Ibid.
5. Lena Dunham, quoted in *Christianity Today*, May 6, 2013, 56.
6. Benjamin Karney, UCLA psychologist and codirector of the Relationship Institute at UCLA.

CHAPTER 8: CLARIFY YOUR LIFE PURPOSE

1. Victor Frankl, *From Death-Camp to Existentialism* (Boston: Beacon Press, 1959), 103.
2. The Westminster Shorter Catechism, New York: P & R Publishing; 2nd edition, 2003.

PART FOUR: CELEBRATING HOPE

1. English *Standard Version* (Wheaton, IL: Cross Way Bibles, 2008), Romans 12:1.

CHAPTER 9: CHOOSE A NEW YOU

1. Behaviorism is a psychological theory maintaining that the study of people should focus on their behavior, not their thoughts and feelings. The Stimulus-Response component of the theory suggests that behavior can be accurately predicted by identifying the stimulus related to the behavior.
2. Norman Cousins, *Human Options* (New York: W. W. Norton Company, 1981), 46, 47.
3. Stephen R. Covey, *7 Habits of Highly Successful People*, New York: Simon & Schuster, 1990.

4. *English Standard Version* (Wheaton, IL: Cross Way Bibles, 2008), Galatians 5:1.

5. *The Message: The Bible in Contemporary Language* (Colorado Springs: NavPress, 2002), 918, Psalm 8:3–4,

6. Blaise Pascal, *Pensees*, translated with an introduction by A. J. Krailsheimer. New York: Penguin Books, 1995.

7. Ibid. "Pascal's Wager" is an argument in apologetic philosophy devised by the seventeenth-century French philosopher, mathematician, and physicist Blaise Pascal (1623–1662). It asserts that all humans bet with their lives either that God exists or does not exist. Given the possibility that God actually does exist and assuming the infinite gain or loss associated with belief in God or with unbelief, a rational person should live as though God exists and seek to believe in God. If God does not actually exist, such a person will have only a finite loss. The philosophy uses the following logic (excerpts from Pensées, part III, §233):

   1. "God is, or He is not."
   2. A Game is being played…where heads or tails will turn up.
   3. According to reason, you can defend neither of the propositions.
   4. You must wager. (It's not optional.)
   5. Let us weigh the gain and the loss in wagering that God is. Let us estimate these two chances. If you gain, you gain all; if you lose, you lose nothing.
   6. Wager, then, without hesitation that He is. (…) There is here an infinity of an infinitely happy life to gain, a chance of gain against a finite number of chances of loss, and what you stake is finite. And so our proposition

is of infinite force, when there is the finite to stake in a game where there are equal risks of gain and of loss, and the infinite to gain.

8. Dean Overman, *A Case for the Existence of God* (Maryland: Rowman & Littlefield Publishers, 2009), xxvi.

9. Malcolm Muggeridge, *Jesus Rediscovered.* Wheaton IL: Tyndale House Publishers, 1979.

10. Ibid.

11. *English Standard Version* (Wheaton, IL: Cross Way Bibles, 2008), Exodus 20:3.

12. See Tim Keller, *The Reason for God* (New York: Dutton, 2008), 168.

13. *English Standard Version* (Wheaton, IL: Cross Way Bibles, 2008), 2 Corinthians 5:17.

14. Archie and Peyton Manning, *Manning,* (New York: Harper Collins Publishers, 2000) 362.

15. Max Weber, German sociologist, philosopher, and political economist, 1846–1920.

16. St. Augustine of Hippo, *Confessions,* an autobiographical work in Latin about AD 397.

17. *English Standard Version* (Wheaton, IL: Cross Way Bibles, 2008), Philippians 4:7.

18. *English Standard Version* (Wheaton, IL: Cross Way Bibles, 2008), Romans 8:31.

19. Marcus Tullius Cicero.

20. *The Message: The Bible in Contemporary Language* (Colorado Springs: NavPress, 2002), Luke 17:14–16.

21. Andrew White, *Faith Under Fire,* Oxford: Monarch, 2011.

22. Andrew White Video

23. *English Standard Version* (Wheaton, IL: Cross Way Bibles, 2008), Psalm 100:1.

24. *English Standard Version* (Wheaton, IL: Cross Way Bibles, 2008), Philippians 4:4.

25. The gospel or good news about the kingdom of God is summarized in John 3:16. Familiar but not always understood, the verse is astonishing. *God*—gospel begins with trust that there is a God. *So loved the world*—everybody. *That He gave His only begotten Son*—God incarnate took upon himself the penalty we could never pay. *That whosoever believes in Him*—a wholehearted trust and commitment available to anyone. *Shall not perish, but have eternal life*—extermination contrasted with life everlasting. The result of this good news when adequately understood is joy (Philippians 4:4).

26. *English Standard Version* (Wheaton, IL: Cross Way Bibles, 2008), Luke 15:10.

27. *English Standard Version* (Wheaton, IL: Cross Way Bibles, 2008), Luke 15:24.

28. *Restless* video link: *www.movingworks.org/project/raised*

29. Sergei prayed this very simple prayer of commitment:

> *Forgive me, Heavenly Father, for trying to live life my way and ignoring your call to follow You. I turn to You now and receive the gift of your relationship with me through faith in Jesus Christ. I want You to be the center of all I think, feel, and do. Transform me according to your will. Amen.*

CHAPTER 10: LIVE WITH THE END IN MIND

1. David Myers, *The Pursuit of Happiness* (New York: William Morrow Paperbacks, 1993), 201.
2. C. S. Lewis, *Surprised By Joy,* New York: Houghton Mifflin Harcourt, 1995.
3. C. S. Lewis quote.
4. Ibid.
5. Reinhold Niebuhr, *Beyond Tragedy*, New York: Charles Scribner's Sons, 1937.
6. *English Standard Version* (Wheaton, IL: Cross Way Bibles, 2008), Colossians 1:11–14.
7. Niebuhr, 20.
8. Ibid, 131.
9. *English Standard Version* (Wheaton, IL: Cross Way Bibles, 2008), John 10:10.
10. N. T. Wright quoted in Tim Keller, *The Reason for God,* 212.
11. English Standard Version (Wheaton, IL: Cross Way Bibles, 2008), Romans 15:13.
12. *English Standard Version* (Wheaton, IL: Cross Way Bibles, 2008), Hebrews 6:19.
13. *Hallelujah* means "Praise God." It's an exclamation of joy.